P9-EER-589

DATE DUE

The Teen-Ager's Menu Cookbook

ALSO BY CHARLOTTE ADAMS

Cooking with Style: Easy, Elegant Recipes &
Menus for Exciting Entertaining

1001 Questions Answered About Cooking

Old Original Bookbinder's Restaurant Cookbook

Easter Idea Book

The Teen-Ager's Menu Cookbook

BY CHARLOTTE ADAMS

DRAWINGS BY
RAGNA TISCHLER GODDARD

Blairsville High School Library

DODD, MEAD & COMPANY
New York

13227 Budget '74

641.5
Ada

Copyright © 1969 by Charlotte Adams
All rights reserved
No part of this book may be reproduced in any form
without permission in writing from the publisher

Fifth Printing

Library of Congress Catalog Card Number: 76–84091
Printed in the United States of America
by The Cornwall Press, Inc., Cornwall, N. Y.

For Margot
with gratitude and love from her
"AUNT FARLEY"

Contents

The Teen-Ager's Menu Cookbook

How to Use This Book

This book is written from the conviction that every boy and every girl who's born into this world alive ought to know how to cook. Not just because the knowledge will be useful for the rest of their lives, which is an excellent reason and utterly true, but because cooking is such fun. It's a truly creative experience with all the satisfaction that writers get from writing, painters from painting—and dancers from dancing, to name just a few. The knowledge that one is able to give pleasure to other people by preparing something delectable to eat is an unbeatable joy, and I couldn't wish you better luck than that you may experience it.

Now for a few pointers on how to use this book. First, carefully read the menu and other material you propose to use at any given time. For example, if a recipe calls for 1 cup of nuts, chopped, that's quite a different thing from 1 cup of chopped nuts. The latter takes more nuts, you see.

Here's the way to use the market lists which accompany each meal. First, nobody should ever go to market without a written shopping list, but it's extraordinary how many people do. So get yourself a piece of paper and first transfer to it all the items on the *Market List*. Then check the staples and whenever you find something missing on the shelves or in the refrigerator, write it down on your list. If you decide to change any item in the menu, go over the recipe you're substituting and check to see whether it requires anything you need to buy. Margarine may always be used in place of butter in the same measurement but, in cooking, it doesn't add as much flavor. You should also cancel out ingredients required for the recipe you're not going to use.

Try to work something out with your family which lets you be responsible for doing the marketing when you're going to be the cook and also for keeping supplies up in the snack department. It will be good experience for you. The ideal way would be to get a weekly budget to cover snacks and then learn to keep yourself within that. It would, I should think, be understood that this is for things you eat at home. It would not cover trips to soda fountains and the like. That comes out of your allowance or money you earn. The snack budget would be a part of the family food budget, advanced to you so that you might learn some good buying habits and be able to exercise your imagination and growing nutritional knowledge, because after all it is necessary for you to eat well—even between meals.

I know that many of you are so obsessed with trying to stay thin that you are inclined to eat nutritionally unbalanced meals. The worst offenders in the country in this respect are teen-age girls, according to government statistics. Naturally, nobody wants to be fat—or should be—but you can, if you're one of those girls, by starving yourself of essential nutrients, set up defects in your system which may not show now, but will rise to plague you while you're still a young woman. So see that, without being in the least bit hypochondriac about it, you eat soundly from the nutritional, the weight, and the sheer pleasure of good food standpoints—all at once.

In connection with the lists of *Utensils Needed,* let me say that some people (including me) like to get at least most of such objects on the counter before starting to cook. If yours is a very tiny kitchen this may not be possible, as there probably isn't much counter space. However, it means that everything is close at hand and can be got out with ease at the moment it's needed.

In connection with the *Timing* instructions given in each chapter, I should like to point out that if there is a technique required, like paring apples or cutting up carrots, for instance, which you have never tried before, perhaps you should allow a little more time to accomplish it than you will need after you've done it once. None of the techniques is complicated, but at the very beginning you can certainly forgive yourself if you take a little longer than the book suggests. Also, in connection with timing, when there is a meat to be cooked which you can do either rare, medium, or well done, I have given the time in accordance with *one* of these stages of doneness. In each case, the recipe which follows tells you how long it takes to cook the meat to all three degrees of doneness. If you prefer one either longer or shorter than that given in the Timing, simply adjust the time schedule to match.

Often recipes tell you to add seasonings "to taste." This means exactly what it says. All good cooks taste the food they're cooking. How else can you tell whether it's just right? Add any seasonings gingerly, taste, and add more if you've been too delicate about it. But remember that it's a lot easier to add more than to subtract when you've put too much in; in fact, the latter is, by and large, impossible.

A timer is one of the most important adjuncts in any kitchen. It allows you to concentrate on other matters while the process you're timing goes on. Sometimes it rings and you say to yourself, "What was *that* for? Oh, yes, the cake's done."—or whatever it may be. When you use a timer well, it keeps the whole situation under control for you.

Don't forget that it's exceedingly important to serve hot food on hot plates and cold food on cold plates. Put dinner plates and those to be used for hot desserts into a warm oven or plate warmer, if you have one. See that they are well warmed, as this helps to keep hot food far more palatable and flavorful. Put plates for salad or cold desserts into the refrigerator to chill them well before they are used. Not only do these things make the food taste better, but they give the people at your table a feeling that you care how your food is presented and how they react to it.

Last of all, let me urge you to use all the help you can get when you give a party. In order to take full advantage of such help you have to be well organized yourself, know exactly what friends can do to expedite the situation, and tell them just what to do and when. If you really have fun cooking, they're bound to enjoy it too.

May you learn to love your kitchen—the pots and pans, the wonderful smells, the delicious food you produce there!

What Does That Mean?

A GLOSSARY OF COOKING TERMS

Bake: To cook in the oven. It is also possible to "bake" pancakes or waffles on top of the range.

Baste: To pour or brush melted fat or liquid over food. The pouring can be done with a spoon, or (much better) with a bulb baster. The object of basting is to keep foods moist and to add flavor.

Beat: To mix briskly with a spoon, rotary beater, wire whisk, or electric beater. A good beating thoroughly mixes all ingredients involved.

Beat lightly: This is a term usually applied to eggs, involving sufficient light beating with a fork to mix yolks and whites completely.

Beat Until Peaks are Formed: This term is applied chiefly to egg whites. Beat with rotary or electric beater until soft peaks are formed when the beater is lifted up through the whites. At this point the beaten whites will still be moist and shiny. It cannot be done with a blender.

Beat Stiff: This term is also applied to egg whites. Beat them with a rotary or electric beater until almost dry and until

7

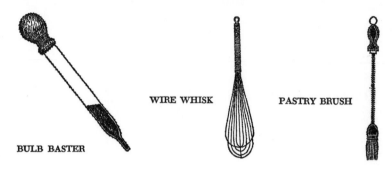

WIRE WHISK   PASTRY BRUSH

BULB BASTER

peaks will hold their shape when the beater is lifted up through the whites. It cannot be done with a blender.

Blend: To mix two or more ingredients together with a spoon and a more gentle motion than is used in beating. A "blender" does a much more vigorous job than is indicated when you are asked to blend ingredients, which is why I always use the term "whirl in the blender," denoting vigorous action.

Boil: To bring liquid to the boiling point (212 degrees F. at sea level). So long as bubbles rise to the top and break, the liquid is boiling. The fastest is known as a "full, rolling boil." The slowest is a low boil which is just barely above a simmer. The term *boil* is also used for cooking foods in boiling water. You are told to *boil* them.

Braise: To brown meat or vegetables in hot fat, then add a small amount of liquid and cook the food, covered, at low heat, usually for a long time.

Broil: To cook under direct heat in a range broiler or portable electric one *or* over direct heat on an open fire or grill.

Brush: To coat food with melted fat or liquid. A pastry brush is most satisfactory to accomplish this job, but if you haven't one you can use a twisted piece of absorbent paper (paper towel).

Caramelize: To melt sugar over low heat, stirring constantly with a wooden spoon until it turns liquid and browns to the degree you want. This requires attention, but is not as tricky as a novice believes.

Chill: To refrigerate a food until it is cold.

Chop: To cut into fine or coarse pieces, as required by the recipe, using a knife or special chopper. Chopped food is never as finely cut as that which is *ground.*

Coat a Spoon: This is a test to indicate that a sauce is done. The desired point is reached when a metal spoon dipped into the sauce comes out coated with some of it.

Cool: To set hot food aside at room temperature until it is no longer hot.

Cream: To mash butter with the back of a spoon until it is creamy. The term "cream the butter and sugar" is also used which simply means that you mix sugar into the butter until the two are thoroughly incorporated into each other and are creamy.

Crisp: To place vegetables in ice water in the refrigerator until crisp and well chilled.

Cube: To cut into small, equal squares.

Cut: To divide food into pieces with a knife or kitchen shears *or* to mix fat into dry ingredients with two knives or a pastry blender, as for making pie crust.

Dredge: To cover food completely with a dry ingredient such as flour or crumbs. It can be done by shaking the food to be dredged in a paper bag with the dry ingredients (and seasonings, if desired), or by using a shaker designed for the purpose.

Fold: To combine two or more ingredients gently with a spoon, a spatula, or the hand. Whichever you use, put it down through the mixture to the bottom of the bowl, across, and up to the top. This is continued until the ingredients are well mixed but still retain air.

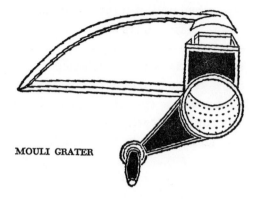

MOULI GRATER

Fry: To cook partly or wholly immersed in fat, either in a skillet containing one or two inches of fat or in a deep-fat fryer with lots of fat. Either of these utensils can be top-of-the-range or electric.

Grate: To pulverize food by rubbing it against a rough surface (a grater), or by using a special grater (like the Mouli). The equivalent result can often be achieved by whirling foods, such as nuts, in the blender.

Grease: To coat a cooking dish or pan with fat. Use either a piece of paper or a pastry brush to accomplish this.

Grill: To broil. The term comes from the rack on which food is cooked in this manner. It is also used to means foods, such as sandwiches, that are cooked with very little fat on a griddle or frying pan.

Grind: To reduce food to small particles, as with a meat grinder, a blender, or a mortar and pestle.

Julienne: Food cut into matchlike strips.

Knead: To fold, turn, and press down on a dough with the hands until it becomes smooth and elastic.

Marinate: To soak food in a marinade, which is a combination of oil, acid (vinegar or lemon juice or wine), and seasonings. This is done to add flavor and, sometimes, to ten-

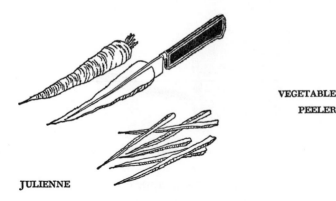

VEGETABLE
PEELER

JULIENNE

derize the food before cooking it. The marinade is often used
in the cooking of the foods that have been soaked in it.

Mince: To cut or chop in very small pieces.

Pan Broil: To cook meat, uncovered, in a hot skillet with no
fat added, pouring off any fat rendered from the meat as it
accumulates.

Pan Fry: To cook, uncovered, in a hot skillet with a very little
fat added.

Parboil: To cook food in boiling water until partially done.
The cooking is usually finished by putting the parboiled,
drained food into a casserole, by frying or sautéeing it, or by
some other means of cooking.

Peel or Pare: To remove an outer skin with a sharp knife or a
vegetable peeler.

Poach: To simmer food gently in a hot liquid.

Purée: To force food through a sieve or food mill or whirl it
in the blender until it is completely smooth.

Roast: To cook in the oven. The term is usually applied to
meat.

Sauté: To cook in a very small amount of hot fat.

Scald: To heat milk or cream to the boiling point without let-

FOOD MILL

ting it boil. A few tiny bubbles will appear on the top when the right point is reached, and also a slight film will shine on it. The surest way to scald without boiling is to do the job in a double boiler.

Score: To make slashes in food with a sharp knife. It can apply to meat, especially the surrounding fat, or to bread and cakes before baking.

Sear: To brown fast over high heat or in a hot oven. The term usually refers to meat. Though searing is rarely used in roasting any more, there are still those who think it adds to flavor and seals in the juices.

Shred: To cut into thin slivers with a sharp knife or a shredder.

SCORING CAKE

Shortening: Any one of many kinds of fat used in a batter or dough to make it "short" (tender). Butter, lard, vegetable oils, margarine, and hydrogenated fats are those most commonly used. Fats differ in shortening powers. In general, a fat has greater shortening power if it has good plasticity or workability. Lard has the greatest, but is usually used in combination with butter, which gives more flavor. Oils, being liquid, lack the plastic quality.

Simmer: To cook gently in liquid below the boiling point. There should be only barely observable bubbles coming to the top of the liquid.

Sizzle: To heat briefly to the point where the fat makes a sizzling sound, shaking the pan frequently so that the contents do not burn.

Sliver: To cut food into thin pieces, as for nuts.

Steam: To cook food, covered, over boiling water which does not touch it. There are special pots for steaming, also racks, which put into any pot, will lift the food above the water. The term is also sometimes used to refer to food cooked in a very little liquid or fat, tightly covered, as with onions to get them "soft, but not brown."

Stir: To blend ingredients with a circular motion. It is less vigorous than beating.

Unmold: To remove food from a mold. If it is a pudding or a gelatin dish, the best method is to put the serving dish on top of the open part of the mold, invert it, and then place a hot, damp cloth on the mold itself, long enough to loosen the contents and not melt it. Let us admit at once that this takes practice. Sometimes it helps to run a blunt-ended knife or a spatula between the food and the mold. This must be done with great care not to break the contents and thus make the unmolded dish less attractive. In the case of the Caramel Ring (see page 99), it is easy to run a knife or spatula around it. You will find that the ring comes out easily and that no heat application is needed.

Whip: As applied to cream this means to beat until it holds definite peaks, but you must be very careful not to overbeat or you will find yourself making butter! Use a rotary or electric beater and check often after the cream begins to thicken. Whipping can be done in a blender, but you must turn it on and off almost constantly to avoid overbeating it. It's quicker than with a beater, but also more tricky.

Family Dinners

Could you cook a dinner? Even if you've never tried before, I think you could manage any of the dinners suggested in this chapter and serve them forth with pride, provided you follow directions carefully and stick to the time schedules. This ought to give you an unbeatable feeling of accomplishment. Furthermore, the experience gained will stand you in very good stead for the rest of your life.

In the five dinners which follow I have arbitrarily assumed that they will be served at seven o'clock. I am well aware that people have dinner at six, or six-thirty, or in the middle of the day on Sunday. So if yours is for six, for instance, just move everything in the *Timing* up an hour and it will all come out right.

You will find here two quite different roasts. There is a dinner based on broiled chops and one in which you "broil" chicken in the oven. The final one sets you on the road to preparing fish well. This should give you a good running start on the variety of entrees you are able to offer.

I have not suggested salad with every menu in this chapter, but if your family are salad buffs you can add a mixed green salad to any one of these meals, or, if you prefer, substitute it for the vegetable indicated.

When the dinner involves long cooking, as with a roast, plan to set the table and get out the china to be warmed or chilled, during some of the time when your roast is cooking. On the other hand, if the meal is more or less of a "short order," quick-cooking proposition, like the fish one, by all means set the table and make other preparations before you start to cook, thus avoiding a mad rush at the end.

MENU I Beef Roasted in Foil
For Six Mashed Potatoes
Spinach with Mushrooms
Hot Hard Rolls
Vanilla Ice Cream with Chocolate Sauce
Coffee   Milk

Market List
3 pounds rolled rump of beef
1 package onion soup mix
2 packages frozen chopped spinach
½ pint sour cream
1 8-ounce can sliced mushrooms
6 hard rolls
½ pint light cream
1 quart vanilla ice cream

Check These Staples
Beef bouillon cube or powdered beef stock
Salt
Pepper
Mashed potato mix
Milk
Semisweet chocolate
Unsweetened chocolate

Utensils Roasting pan
Needed Double boiler
Measuring cup
Stirring spoons
Saucepan for spinach
Strainer
Saucepan for potatoes
Pan for heating rolls
Ice cream scoop

TIMING *If dinner is to be served at 7*

4:15 Prepare roast for cooking.

4:20 Preheat oven to 350 degrees.

4:30 Put roast into oven.

6:00 Make chocolate sauce and hold over hot water.

6:30 Cook spinach, drain, add sour cream and mushrooms, and heat.

6:45 Make mashed potatoes.

6:50 Place rolls in oven to heat.

7:00 Put meat onto a heated platter. Pour juices over it.

Put the mashed potatoes in a heated serving dish and rolls in a napkin on a serving plate. Take all to the dining room with heated plates.

When the main course is finished, serve ice cream in chilled bowls and chocolate sauce in a sauce boat so that each person can help himself.

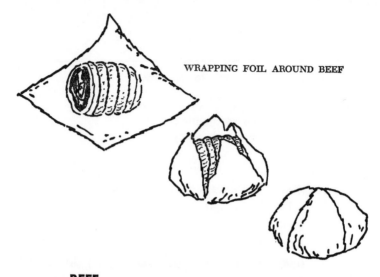

WRAPPING FOIL AROUND BEEF

BEEF ROASTED IN FOIL

3 pounds rolled rump of beef
1 package onion soup mix
½ cup beef stock (made from bouillon cube or powdered beef stock)

Put beef on a large piece of heavy-duty foil. Sprinkle soup mix over the meat. Begin to bring up the sides of the foil and pour in the stock. Fold the meat well in the foil so that it is entirely covered on all sides and well sealed to keep in the juices. Place in a roasting pan and roast in 350 degree oven 2½ hours. *Serves 6.*

CHOCOLATE SAUCE

6 squares semisweet chocolate
1 square unsweetened chocolate
¾ cup light cream

Place chocolate in the top of a double boiler over hot water, cover, and let it melt completely. Stir until smooth. Add cream and stir until completely mixed with the chocolate. Makes about a cup. This keeps very well in a covered jar in the refrigerator.

SPINACH WITH MUSHROOMS

2 packages frozen chopped spinach
½ cup sour cream
1 8-ounce can sliced mushrooms, drained

Cook spinach according to package directions. Drain very well. Mix with sour cream and drained mushrooms. Place over low heat until heated through. *Serves 6.*

MASHED POTATOES

One of the best packaged dehydrated foods in existence is mashed, or "whipped," potatoes. Follow the package directions for excellent results in jig time.

HOT HARD ROLLS

Put the rolls into the oven on a cookie sheet. Ten minutes should heat them well. Remove them and place them on a serving plate, wrapped in a napkin to hold the heat.

MENU II	Broiled Lamb Chops
For Four	New Potatoes
	Green Peas
	Rosemary French Bread
	Floating Island
	Coffee Milk

Market List
4 loin lamb chops, cut 1½″ thick
8 medium-sized new potatoes (or more, if tiny)
2 packages frozen peas
1 package brown-and-serve French bread (freeze the unused loaf)
Fresh parsley, if desired, for potatoes

Check These Staples
Eggs (3)
Milk (2 cups)
Sugar
Salt
Pepper
Vanilla
Superfine sugar
Butter (1½ sticks)
Chicken bouillon cube (1)
Rosemary

Utensils Needed
Measuring cup
Measuring spoons
Double boiler
Small bowl for egg yolks
Fork or wire whisk

Metal stirring spoon
Large bowl for beating egg whites
Saucepan for cooking potatoes
Small saucepan for melting butter
Pan or cookie sheet for baking bread
Flat knife or spatula for spreading butter
Saucepan for cooking peas
Strainer

TIMING *If dinner is to be served at 7*

In the morning, or early enough in the afternoon to chill it thoroughly, at least 2 hours, make the Floating Island.

6:15 Prepare rosemary French bread.
6:25 Prepare potatoes.
6:30 Season chops and place on broiler pan.
6:35 Cook potatoes. Drain. Keep warm.
6:36 Preheat broiler to 350 degrees.
6:40 Cook peas. Drain. Add butter.
6:45 Put bread into oven.
6:46 Put chops into broiler.
6:51 Turn chops (for rare).
6:55 Pour hot melted butter over potatoes.
6:56 Remove chops from broiler.
6:57 Sizzle peas.
Serve the dinner.
After the main course has been eaten, serve the Floating Island.

FLOATING ISLAND
2 cups milk
1 whole egg

2 egg yolks (To separate yolks from whites
        see page 199.)
3 tablespoons sugar
Dash salt
½ teaspoon vanilla
2 egg whites
¼ cup superfine sugar

Place milk in top of double boiler over hot water and heat until milk is hot, but not boiling. There will be a slight film over the surface when it is ready. This is called *scalding*. Combine the whole egg with the egg yolks in a bowl and beat them slightly with a fork or a wire whisk. Stir in salt and sugar. Stir into hot milk and cook over the hot water, stirring constantly with a metal spoon until thickened. The custard will cling to the spoon when you lift it up if it is properly done. Add vanilla and cool. Beat the egg whites with the superfine sugar to make a *meringue*. (They should be stiff and form peaks when you lift them up with the beater.) Pour the cool custard into four individual serving bowls or dishes. Top each with ¼ of the meringue. Chill until ready to serve. *Serves 4.*

ROSEMARY
FRENCH
BREAD

1 loaf brown-and-serve French bread
¼ cup (½ stick) softened butter
½ teaspoon dried rosemary

Take the butter out of the refrigerator ½ hour before you want to use it. Slice the bread from the top not quite down to the bottom crust in ½-inch slices. Mix butter and rosemary

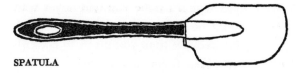

SPATULA

well and, with a flat knife or spatula, spread it between the
slices, trying not to break the loaf apart where you've made
your cuts. However, if it does come apart in one or two
places, do not despair, just press it together again. If there
is any butter left over, spread it on top of the loaf. Place on
a pan or cookie sheet. Bake according to package directions
until lightly brown and hot (12–15 minutes). *Serves 4.*

NEW POTATOES

8 new potatoes (or more)
¼ cup (½ stick) melted butter
Parsley, if desired

Scrub the potatoes and cook in boiling, salted water until
done (about 10–15 minutes, depending upon their size).
Serve in their jackets (which make delicious eating) with
melted butter poured over them. Decorate with sprigs of
parsley for a prettier dish. *Serves 4.*

BROILED LAMB CHOPS

4 loin lamb chops, 1½″ thick
Salt and pepper

Sprinkle chops with salt and pepper. Place on broiler pan 3
inches from 350 degree heat. Cook 5–6 minutes per side for
rare, 7–8 minutes per side for medium, and 9–10 minutes per

side for well done, which I hope you will never want to do. Lamb chops should be at least faintly pink to be delicious. Set your timer for half the time you mean to cook the chops and when it rings, turn them and set for other half of the cooking. *Serves 4.*

GREEN
PEAS

2 packages frozen green peas
½ cup water
1 chicken bouillon cube
¼ cup (½ stick) butter

Bring water to the boil and dissolve bouillon cube in it. Add peas and break up with a fork. Cook until just tender (5–7 minutes) and drain. Put butter into pan, return drained peas to it and when ready to serve turn on moderate heat under the pan until peas and butter sizzle a little (about 1 minute). *Serves 4–6.*

FUTURES

In learning how to make Floating Island you have achieved the ability to make soft custard, which is a basic sauce for many dishes and a very useful "dresser-upper" for stale cake, for instance.

MENU III Roast Loin of Pork
For Four Horseradish Applesauce
Boat Potatoes
Candied Carrots
Oven Toast
Ginger Cookie Roll
Coffee   Milk

Market List Ginger cookies (12)
½ pint heavy cream
Pork loin containing 8 chops
4 baking potatoes
Grated Parmesan cheese or slabs of Cheddar
    cheese
8 carrots
1 8-ounce jar applesauce

**Check These
Staples** Vanilla
Superfine sugar
Salt
Pepper
Butter (1½ sticks)
Paprika
Brown sugar
Bottled horseradish
White bread (6 slices)

**Utensils
Needed** Bowl for cream
Measuring spoons
Rotary or electric beater
Spatulas or knives for spreading

Utensils	Roasting pan and rack
Needed	Meat thermometer
(cont.)	Vegetable scraper or sharp paring knife
	Bowl to hold carrots in water
	Bowl for mixing applesauce
	Saucepan for cooking carrots
	Strainer
	Skillet for glazing carrots
	Cookie sheet

TIMING   *If dinner is to be served at 7*

At least 4 hours before dinner, make Ginger Cookie Roll. You may do it the night before if that's more convenient.

4:05   Preheat oven to 350 degrees.

4:10   Prepare pork for roasting.

4:15   Place pork in oven.

5:25   Scrub potatoes.

5:30   Place potatoes in oven.

5:35   Prepare carrots for cooking and put into a bowl of cold water until ready to cook.

6:00   Make horseradish applesauce.

6:15   Prepare bread for baking.

6:30   Put bread into oven.

6:30   Test potatoes and if soft, remove from oven and finish preparation. Return to oven.

6:35   Cook carrots. Drain. Glaze them as recipe indicates.

Serve the dinner.

When the first course is finished, serve the Ginger Cookie Roll.

GINGER COOKIE ROLL

GINGER
COOKIE ROLL

12 thin ginger cookies
½ pint heavy cream
¼ teaspoon vanilla
2 tablespoons superfine sugar

Whip the cream (see page 201) and flavor with vanilla and sugar. Spread one side of a cookie with whipped cream and place another one against it. Spread the second cookie and add another. Continue the process until cookies are used up. Stand the roll of cookies on edge on a plate or small platter as you do this and finish by spreading whipped cream over the roll thus made. Place in the refrigerator for at least four hours before serving. Cut the roll for serving at an angle so that each slice consists of stripes of cream and ginger. *Serves 4–6.*

ROAST LOIN
OF PORK

1 pork loin containing eight chops
Salt and pepper

Have the butcher cut the backbone from the ribs and tie it to the roast. It should be removed after roasting for easier carving. Place the roast on a rack in a roasting pan. Season with salt and pepper. Roast in 350 degree oven 35–40 minutes per pound or until meat thermometer reaches 185 degrees. Remove from the oven and let stand a few minutes on a hot platter so that the juices can settle. *Serves 4.*

BOAT POTATOES

4 baking potatoes
6 tablespoons butter
Grated Parmesan cheese or slabs of Cheddar cheese
Paprika

Because you are cooking the pork roast these potatoes will be cooked at 350 degrees (usually it would be at higher heat), so they must also cook longer than usual, but they will come out just as well. Scrub the potatoes and place them in the oven. Cook an hour or more, or until soft when squeezed or pierced with a fork. If you squeeze them, be sure to do it with a potholder or you'll be burned! Remove from the oven and split down the middle. Take out soft insides with a fork and break up well, adding butter. Return to potato shells and either sprinkle with grated Parmesan or lay a slab of Cheddar on each. Sprinkle with paprika. Return to oven until (if grated) cheese browns or (if slabs) melts. *Serves 4.*

CANDIED CARROTS

8 carrots
2 tablespoons butter
2 tablespoons brown sugar

Scrape carrots. I hope you have a vegetable scraper. Otherwise, use a sharp paring knife. Cut into sticks (first cut each carrot in half and then cut the halves into sticks). Plunge into boiling, salted water and cook until just tender (test with a fork). Drain well. Melt butter in skillet. Add carrots and stir so that all are coated. Sprinkle on brown sugar and cook over low heat, stirring occasionally, until sugar melts and glazes the carrots. *Serves 4.*

HORSERADISH APPLESAUCE

1 8-ounce jar applesauce
Bottled grated horseradish to taste

Put applesauce into a bowl, add horseradish a little at a time and stir it in well, tasting as you go to get exactly the flavor you like. Remember, it's better to underseason than to add too much of a sharp flavor at the start. *Serves 4.*

OVEN TOAST

6 slices white bread
¼ cup (½ stick) butter

Remove crusts from bread. Butter each slice amply on one side. Cut each into 2 triangles. Place, unbuttered side down, on a cookie sheet. Place in oven with roast and cook until golden brown (about 30 minutes). *Serves 4.*

MENU IV   Oven "Broiled" Chicken

For Four   Chicken Gravy

Dry Rice

Chopped Spinach

Pears   Cheese

Coffee   Milk

Market List
1 3-pound broiler-fryer, split but not cut up
1 package chicken gravy mix
2 packages frozen chopped spinach
½ pint sour cream
4 ripe pears
Bel Paese or other cheese of your choice

Check These Staples
Salt
Pepper
Flour
Butter (½ stick)
Converted rice (1 cup)
Nutmeg

Utensils Needed
Roasting pan with rack
Measuring cup
Bulb baster
Fork for pricking chicken
Saucepan with tight-fitting lid for rice
Measuring spoons
Saucepan for spinach
Stirring spoon
Skillet
Flour shaker
Strainer

TIMING   *If dinner is to be served at 7*

5:55   Preheat oven to 400 degrees.

5:56   Prepare chicken for cooking.

6:05   Place chicken in the oven. *Don't forget to baste about every ten minutes.*

6:30   Bring water and salt to boil for rice.

6:35   Add rice and cook according to recipe.

6:40   Cook spinach. You can keep it warm over the hot water until ready to serve.

6:50   Remove chicken from roasting pan and keep warm in turned-off oven.

6:51   Make chicken gravy.
        Serve the dinner.
        When first course is finished, serve pears and cheese.

**OVEN-
BROILED
CHICKEN**   1 3-pound broiler-fryer, split (not cut up)
             Salt and pepper
             Flour
             ¼ cup (½ stick) butter
             ½ cup water

Wipe chicken with a damp cloth. Place, skin side up, on a rack in a roasting pan. Sprinkle with salt and pepper. Sprinkle lightly with flour (easiest to do with a flour shaker). Dot with butter. Pour a little water into the pan and bake in 400 degree oven 45 minutes or until done, basting frequently with liquid in pan. Test for doneness by pricking the meatiest part of the leg with a fork. If the juice which runs out is yellow, the chicken is done. If it is pink, a little more cooking is needed. But never overcook it or it will become dry and stringy. Keep warm on hot platter in turned-off oven while making gravy. *Serves 4.*

**DRY
RICE** 1 cup converted rice
2 cups water
1 teaspoon salt

Bring water, with salt, to the boil. Gradually add rice. When it reaches the boil again, reduce heat very low, cover the pot tightly and cook 25 minutes, or until all the water is absorbed. *Serves 4.*

**CHOPPED
SPINACH** 2 packages frozen chopped spinach
½ cup sour cream
Dash nutmeg

Cook spinach according to package directions just until it is hot through (about 3 minutes). Drain very thoroughly. Mix with sour cream and nutmeg and place saucepan in a skillet of hot water to reheat to piping. *Serves 4–6.*

**CHICKEN
GRAVY** 1 package chicken gravy mix
Pan drippings
1 cup cold water

Pour contents of package of chicken gravy mix into the drippings in the roasting pan. Gradually add water and cook on top of the range, stirring constantly, until thickened and smooth. Serve in a gravy boat. *Serves 4.*

PEARS AND CHEESE

There's no easier or more delectable dessert than pears with cheese. Any kind of cheese you enjoy is all right with pears, but I'd like to suggest that the Italian Bel Paese has perhaps the greatest affinity for this fruit, so perhaps you'd like to try that.

MENU V	Fried Butterfish
For Four	Potato Puffs
	Salad Mimosa
	Butterfly Rolls
	Brownies
	Coffee Milk

Market List	4 ½-pound butterfish
	Fresh parsley
	1 package frozen potato puffs
	1 large head Boston lettuce
	1 package Butterfly rolls
	⅓ pound walnuts (about)

Check These Staples	Salt
	Pepper
	Flour
	Eggs (5)
	Dry breadcrumbs
	Butter (1¼ stick)
	Lemons
	Olive oil
	Vinegar
	Unsweetened chocolate (2 squares)
	Sugar
	Vanilla
	Milk

Utensils Needed	Mixing bowl
	Measuring cups
	Measuring spoons
	Beating spoon
	Rotary or electric beater
	Shallow 9" pan for brownies
	Knife to cut brownies
	Cookie sheet for rolls
	Clean tea towel
	Skillet for frying fish
	Flour shaker
	Bowl for egg and water
	Platter for breadcrumbs
	Paring knife
	Cookie sheet for potato puffs
	Chopper for egg whites
	Grater for egg yolks
	Salad bowl

TIMING *If dinner is to be served at 7*

In the morning (or at least early enough to chill them thoroughly—2 hours) hardcook 2 eggs (see page 199) for the salad.

Make the brownies as early as possible so

they can cool to room temperature for serving.

6:30   Preheat oven to 425 degrees.

6:31   Prepare fish for cooking.

6:40   Put potato puffs into oven (peek at them occasionally to be sure they reach the degree of crisp brownness you like).

6:41   Make salad.

6:50   Put rolls into oven to heat.

6:51   Fry fish.

Serve dinner.

When first course is finished, serve brownies and coffee together.

BROWNIES

2 squares unsweetened chocolate
1 cup sugar
Dash salt
¼ cup (½ stick) butter
2 egg yolks
½ teaspoon vanilla
¼ cup milk
⅔ cup flour
2 egg whites, beaten stiff
1 cup chopped walnuts

Melt chocolate in a mixing bowl over a saucepan of hot water. Add sugar, salt, and butter. Mix well. When cool, add egg yolks and beat thoroughly. Add vanilla, milk, half of the flour, beaten egg whites, nuts, and remaining flour. Pour into a greased shallow pan about 9″ square and bake 40 minutes in a 250 degree oven. Cool to room temperature. Cut into squares to serve.

FRIED
BUTTERFISH

4 ½-pound butterfish
Salt and pepper
Flour
1 egg
1 tablespoon water
1 cup dry breadcrumbs
6 tablespoons butter
4 lemon wedges
Fresh parsley

Season fish with salt and pepper and dredge with flour (from a shaker, if you have one). Beat egg with water. Dip fish into this mixture, then into breadcrumbs. This will be easiest if you spread the crumbs on a platter or a piece of foil. Melt butter in a skillet and fry the fish in it until well browned on one side. Turn and brown the other side. This should take not more than about 2 minutes to a side, otherwise the fish will be dry and overcooked. Serve at once on a hot platter with lemon wedges and parsley sprigs. *Serves 4.*

POTATO
PUFFS

1 package frozen potato puffs

Cook puffs according to package directions in a 425 degree oven. If you like them crisp, cook longer than the 12 minutes indicated (I do mine about 20 minutes). *Serves 4.*

SALAD
MIMOSA

1 large head Boston lettuce
¼ cup olive oil

1 tablespoon vinegar
½ teaspoon salt
Dash pepper
2 hard-cooked eggs (see page 199)

Well ahead of time, wash lettuce, shake to remove excess water, wrap in a clean tea towel and store in the refrigerator to crisp. When ready to make salad, tear lettuce into pieces into a salad bowl. Mix oil, vinegar, salt, and pepper. Pour over the greens. Chop the egg whites coarsely. Add to lettuce and toss well. Grate the egg yolks over the top of the salad. *Serves 4–6.*

BUTTERFLY ROLLS

Buy these in a package. Heat well before serving in a 425 degree oven for about 8–10 minutes.

FUTURES

In learning how to panfry fish you have another basic cooking technique under your belt. Trout, sole, porgies, dabs, and smelt are all fine cooked in this manner. Any of them, by the way, can be rolled in cornmeal instead of breadcrumbs for a change of flavor.

Casserole Dinners

Some of the best dishes ever invented are made from leftover foods. And that, in essence, is what this chapter is all about. I make specific suggestions in each case, just to help you get into the swing of looking into the refrigerator to see what bits and pieces are available and then going on to improvise, use your imagination, and come up with original and delicious dishes of your own creation.

There are a few basic principles to keep in mind. By and large it is not a good idea to add leftover beets to a casserole, for they will turn the whole dish red and most of the time that's not appetizing. They are, however, very tasty when put into corned beef hash before browning it (thus making it a Red Flannel Hash) or cut into thin strips and mixed into a green salad (which makes it a Chiffonade Salad). If you have a few delicate peas among your leftovers it is not a good idea to combine them in a casserole with a member of the cabbage family (cabbage, broccoli, Brussels sprouts, cauliflower) as their flavor will be completely overpowered. On the other hand, if you found a few cooked carrots, green beans, and peas—and perhaps some corn—in the refrigerator, they would combine perfectly in a good sauce, either as a vegetable casserole or mixed with meat for a complete one-dish meal.

As for the sauces you use in casseroles, canned soups are a blessing with no disguise at all. I happen to think that mushroom soup is the best, as it combines well with almost everything. But lots of times tomato is precisely the thing you need most to give your leftovers color and a lift. You can dilute the soups for sauces with either milk or water. I prefer milk or sometimes light cream if richness is what I'm after. Never dilute soup for a sauce as much as you would if you were going to use it as soup. It will thin out in the cooking of the casserole and become entirely too liquid for most people's taste in sauces. There are also many excellent sauce mixes which come in flat envelopes and are very easy to store, since they take up so little room on the shelf.

Always investigate everything in the refrigerator with an eye to incorporating it into any casserole you're making. For instance, if I make Hollandaise sauce and there is even a tiny bit left over (a tablespoonful or so), I save it and put it into any casserole with any kind of sauce at all. Even that small amount of Hollandaise improves the flavor of anything you incorporate it into. So if your mother is not in the habit of saving such tiny "dribs and drabs," beg her to help you improve your inventive skill by doing so!

As a rule, you will probably be most interested in making casserole meals which need only salad and perhaps bread, plus dessert, to round them out. This means that you want a protein (fish, meat, or poultry), a starch usually (rice, potato, pasta, and the like) and some vegetables which you make especially delectable by inventing a splendid sauce. Often it's a good idea to start with a basic cream sauce (see page 197) and add special seasonings to it. As always, taste as you go and add herbs, spices, onion, ketchup, chili sauce, or whatever else you think will turn leftovers into a delicious dish. And never forget the rule which says that when you're experimenting with seasonings, be conservative about it, tasting as you go until you get exactly the flavor you think is best. If you wildly dump in too much there's no satisfactory way to get the flavor out of your dish.

Here's a series of menus based on leftovers, sometimes combined with other leftovers, sometimes dressed up with something you cook especially to put into the casseroles in which each of them is cooked.

CASSEROLE **DINNER I**	(Using leftover meat loaf)
For Four	Tamale Pie
	Chiffonade Salad
	Applesauce Ginger Cookies
	Coffee Milk

Market List	1 8-ounce can tomato sauce
	1 12-ounce can whole kernel corn
	1 head Boston lettuce
Check These **Staples**	Leftover meat loaf
	Onions (1)
	Garlic
	Bacon (or other) fat
	Chili powder
	Salt
	Pepper
	Green olives (6)
	Yellow cornmeal (1 cup)
	Cheddar cheese (3 tablespoons, grated)
	Butter

Check These
Staples
(cont.)
Leftover or canned beets (1 cup cut in sticks)
Olive oil
Vinegar
1 1-pound jar applesauce
Ginger cookies (or make from recipe on page
190)

Utensils
Needed
Chopper for onion and garlic
Measuring spoons
Measuring cups
Good-sized frying pan
Fork for stirring
Saucepan for cornmeal mush
Stirring spoon
Baking dish
Cheese grater
Clean tea towel
Bowl for mixing salad dressing
Salad bowl
Salad fork and spoon

TIMING

If dinner is to be served at 7

Well ahead of time wash lettuce, shake to remove excess moisture, and refrigerate it in a clean tea towel. If you're going to make the cookies yourself, do that well ahead also.

6:00 Prepare tamale pie.

6:20 Preheat oven to 350 degrees.

6:30 Put tamale pie in oven.

6:45 Put the salad together.

Serve the dinner.

When the first course is finished, serve the applesauce and cookies.

TAMALE PIE

1 medium onion
1 clove garlic
2 tablespoons bacon (or other) fat
3 cups crumbled cold meat loaf
1 8-ounce can tomato sauce
1 teaspoon chili powder
½ teaspoon salt
Pepper to taste
1 12-ounce can whole kernel corn
6 green olives, sliced
1 cup yellow cornmeal
4 cups boiling water
½ teaspoon salt
3 tablespoons grated Cheddar cheese
Butter for dotting

CHOPPER FOR ONION AND GARLIC

Chop onion and garlic coarsely and fry in bacon fat until golden. Add crumbled meat loaf and cook over medium heat, stirring with a fork to keep the meat broken up, for about 5 minutes. Add tomato sauce, corn, olives and seasonings and simmer on low heat. Cook cornmeal in the boiling water with salt added for 5 minutes, stirring constantly. Line the bottom and sides of a baking dish with this mush, saving enough to cover the top of the dish. Pour in the meat mixture and cover with mush. Sprinkle with cheese and dot with butter. Bake in 350 degree oven until nicely brown on top (about 30 minutes). *Serves 4 generously.*

Note: This dish can be made from scratch, using 1 pound of chopped beef in place of leftover meat loaf.

CHIFFONADE
SALAD

1 head Boston lettuce
1 cup julienne (see page 10) beets
5 tablespoons olive oil
2 tablespoons vinegar
Salt and pepper to taste

Well ahead of time wash the lettuce, shake to remove excess moisture, wrap in a clean tea towel, and place in the refrigerator to crisp. When ready to serve, tear the lettuce into a salad bowl. Add beets. Mix oil, vinegar, salt and pepper and pour over lettuce and beets. Toss well with a salad fork and spoon. *Serves 4.*

APPLESAUCE

Since excellent applesauce comes in jars, it is my feeling that they should be part of the staple shelf. When you know you're going to use it for dessert, put a jar in the refrigerator in the morning to be sure it will be nice and cold at dinner time. If your family likes it that way, serve light cream or half-and-half to pour over it.

GINGER
COOKIES

If you're in the mood to make cookies yourself, you'll find a recipe on page 190. Otherwise, as you know, there are excellent ginger cookies to be bought packaged.

CASSEROLE DINNER II
For Four

(Using leftover lamb, carrots, peas, and mashed potato, if available)

Shepherd's Pie
Orange and Onion Salad
Rye Crisp
Chocolate French Toast
Coffee   Milk

Market List

1 can condensed mushroom soup
Iceberg lettuce
3 navel oranges
1 large red onion
Rye Crisp

Check These Staples

Leftover lamb (2 cups)
Cooked or canned onions (1 cup)
Cooked diced carrots (1 cup)
Cooked or canned peas (1 cup)
Rosemary
Milk
Mashed potatoes (2 cups)
Butter (½ stick)
Olive oil
Vinegar
Salt
Pepper
White bread (4 slices)
Semisweet chocolate (4 squares)

Utensils   Measuring cups
Needed   Casserole
           Clean tea towel
           Paring knife
           Small bowl for mixing salad dressing
           Measuring spoons
           Skillet for French toast

TIMING   *If dinner is to be served at 7*

Well ahead of time wash lettuce, separating leaves, shake to remove excess water, wrap in a clean tea towel and place in refrigerator to crisp.

6:00   Prepare casserole, cooking vegetables if necessary and making mashed potatoes if necessary.

6:20   Preheat oven to 350 degrees.

6:30   Put casserole into oven.

6:35   Prepare orange and onion salad.

6:50   Put salad together.

7:00   Serve dinner.

After the first course is finished, make the French toast. It's a "short order" dessert, so can't be made ahead of time, but it takes only about ten minutes and no one will mind waiting to have it served perfectly.

SHEPHERD'S PIE

This recipe takes for granted that you have leftover lamb or you would not be making the dish. If you were lucky ·

enough to find in the refrigerator also some cooked onions, carrots, peas, and mashed potatoes you'd have practically no work left to do! Otherwise, you might add canned onions, peas, and carrots or cook up a package of frozen peas and carrots and mix them with canned onions for the dish, and make your mashed potatoes from a packaged mix.

> 2 cups cooked lamb, cubed
> 1 cup cooked or canned onions
> 1 cup cooked diced carrots
> 1 cup cooked or canned peas
> ½ teaspoon rosemary
> 1 can condensed mushroom soup
> ½ cup milk
> 2 cups mashed potatoes
> Butter for dotting

Combine lamb, onions, carrots, peas, rosemary, soup, and milk in a casserole and mix well. Top with mashed potatoes. Dot with butter. Bake in 375 degree oven until top is brown (about 30 minutes). *Serves 4.*

ORANGE AND ONION SALAD

> 8 leaves iceberg lettuce
> 3 navel oranges
> 1 large red onion
> 4 tablespoons olive oil
> 1 tablespoon vinegar
> Salt and pepper to taste

Wash lettuce well ahead of serving time, shake to remove excess moisture, wrap in a clean tea towel, and crisp in the refrigerator. When ready to prepare the salad, peel the oranges, being sure to remove all the white "zest" under the skin. Cut into thin slices, removing any seeds. Peel the onion and slice it into very thin rings. Arrange two leaves of lettuce on each of four salad plates. Place slices of orange and onion on them. Mix oil, vinegar, salt and pepper and sprinkle over the salads. *Serves 4.*

RYE
CRISP

The rye crisp is suggested because this is more or less a soft meal and needs a little crunch for interesting texture contrast.

CHOCOLATE
FRENCH
TOAST

4 slices white bread
4 tablespoons butter (or more, if needed)
4 squares semisweet chocolate

Spread half the butter on one side of each slice of bread. Melt remaining butter in a skillet. Place the bread, buttered side up, in the skillet. Cook over moderate heat until bottom is golden. Meantime, break or slice chocolate into small pieces, or shave it with a vegetable peeler. Turn bread slices when ready and place chocolate on top. Cook until chocolate melts and under side of bread is golden. *Serves 4.*

**CASSEROLE
DINNER III**   (Using leftover Cooked Fish)
For Four   Norwegian Fish Pudding
                  Shrimp Sauce
                  Frozen Peas
                  Hot Hard Rolls
                  Bread Pudding
                  Coffee   Milk

Market List   1 can frozen cream of shrimp soup
                  2 packages frozen peas
                  4–8 hard rolls

Check These   Cooked fish (2 cups)
Staples   Eggs (4 and 2 whites)
                  Pepper
                  Nutmeg
                  Cornstarch
                  Salt
                  Cream (¾ cup, plus)
                  Milk (1 quart, plus 1½ cups)
                  Sherry
                  Chicken bouillon cube or powdered stock
                  White bread (6 slices)
                  Butter (½ stick)
                  Sugar
                  Vanilla

Utensils Needed	Blender or grinder
	Bowl for mixing fish pudding

Utensils
Needed
Blender or grinder
Bowl for mixing fish pudding
Measuring cups
Measuring spoons
Electric mixer or rotary beater
Loaf pan
Saucepan for sauce
Saucepan for peas
Strainer
Cooky sheet
Knife for buttering
Double boiler
Bowl for mixing bread pudding
Baking dish
Can opener
Pan of hot water

TIMING *If dinner is to be served at 7*
5:30 Make fish pudding.
5:50 Preheat oven to 350 degrees.
6:00 Put fish pudding into oven.
6:01 Put milk for bread pudding on to scald.
6:05 Defrost shrimp soup as directed.
6:10 Make bread pudding.
6:30 Make shrimp sauce.
6:40 Put rolls into oven.
6:45 Put bread pudding into oven.
6:50 Cook peas.
Serve dinner.

A half hour has been allowed for eating the first course, at which point the bread pudding will be done. If yours is a family of speedy eaters, perhaps you'd prefer to put the dessert into the oven sooner.

NORWEGIAN FISH PUDDING

2 cups cooked solid-meat fish (cod, halibut, haddock, salmon)
2 egg whites
Dash pepper
Dash nutmeg
½ teaspoon cornstarch
½ teaspoon salt
½ cup cream
1½ cups milk

Put the fish, broken up, and the egg whites into the blender and whirl until completely blended. *Or* put them through the finest blade of the grinder at least twice. Add pepper, nutmeg, cornstarch, and salt and mix well. Beat with electric mixer or rotary beater, gradually adding cream and milk, until very smooth (about 15 minutes). Pour into a greased loaf pan and bake in a 350 degree oven for 1 hour. Slice to serve. *Serves four.*

SHRIMP SAUCE

1 can frozen cream of shrimp soup
¼ to ⅓ cup cream
1 tablespoon sherry (optional)

Thaw the soup by placing the unopened can in a pan of hot water for about 30 minutes. Open can and put soup in a saucepan, adding enough cream to make it the consistency you like. Add sherry, if desired, and heat well. Serve in a sauce boat so that each person may take as much as he likes for his fish pudding.

FROZEN
PEAS   2 packages frozen peas

Cook peas according to package directions. Drain. Put back into saucepan with a good hunk of butter and sizzle a little before serving, shaking the pan frequently. You may give added flavor to the peas by cooking them in chicken stock, made from a bouillon cube or powdered stock. *Serves 4–6* (you will probably have some leftovers).

HOT
HARD ROLLS

Place hard rolls on a cookie sheet and heat in 350 degree oven along with the fish pudding until piping (15–20 minutes). Serve wrapped in a napkin to retain heat.

BREAD
PUDDING   6 slices bread
¼ cup (½ stick) soft butter
4 eggs, well beaten
¼ cup sugar
½ teaspoon vanilla
Dash nutmeg
1 quart milk, scalded (see page 11)

Cut crusts from bread, and butter each slice on one side.

Combine eggs, sugar, vanilla, and nutmeg. Add the scalded milk gradually to the egg mixture, stirring until the sugar is dissolved. Pour into a baking dish and put bread on top, buttered side up. Place in a pan of hot water and bake in 350 degree oven until firm (45–50 minutes). Serve hot with cream to pour over, if desired. *Serves 4 to 6.*

CASSEROLE DINNER IV   (Using leftover ham)
For Four   Ham and Macaroni
Frenched Green Beans
Butterscotch Ice Cream Cake
Coffee   Milk

Market List   8 ounces elbow macaroni
2 packages frozen Frenched green beans

Check These Staples   Butter (about 1 stick)
Flour
Milk (1½ cups)
Cream (½ cup)
Salt
Pepper
Cubed cooked ham (1 cup)
Grated Parmesan cheese (½ cup)
Brown sugar (1 cup)
Light corn syrup (⅔ cup)
Pound cake (4 slices)
Vanilla ice cream (4 scoops)

Utensils Saucepan for macaroni
Needed Strainer
Saucepan for making sauce for casserole
Measuring cups
Measuring spoons
Casserole
Cheese grater
Saucepan for cooking beans
Small saucepan for making dessert sauce

TIMING *If dinner is to be served at 7*
6:15 Cook macaroni.
6:16 Make sauce for casserole.
6:20 Preheat oven to 375 degrees.
6:24 Drain macaroni.
6:25 Put casserole together.
6:30 Put casserole into oven.
6:35 Make butterscotch sauce.
6:45 Cook beans according to package directions.
Serve dinner.
When first course is finished, serve Butterscotch Ice Cream Cake.

**HAM AND
MACARONI
CASSEROLE**
8 ounces elbow macaroni
6 tablespoons butter
6 tablespoons flour
1½ cups milk
½ cup cream
Salt and pepper to taste
1 cup cubed cooked ham
½ cup grated Parmesan cheese

Cook macaroni in boiling, salted water for 9 minutes. Drain well. Melt butter and stir in flour smoothly. Add milk and cream and cook, stirring constantly, until smooth and thick. Season to taste with salt and pepper. Add macaroni and ham and mix well. Put into a casserole and sprinkle cheese over the top. Bake in 375 degree oven 30 minutes. *Serves 4.*

FRENCHED GREEN BEANS

2 packages frozen Frenched green beans
Butter

Cook beans according to package directions. Drain well. Put a good hunk of butter into the same pan in which the beans were cooked. Add drained beans and sizzle a little before serving. *Serves 4–6.*

BUTTERSCOTCH ICE CREAM CAKE

1 cup brown sugar
⅔ cup light corn syrup
¼ cup (½ stick) butter
½ cup light cream
4 slices pound cake
4 scoops vanilla ice cream

Put sugar, syrup, and butter into a small saucepan and bring to the boil, stirring to be sure that it does not burn. Continue boiling until mixture forms a soft ball when a little is dropped into cold water (235–240 degrees on the candy thermometer). Remove from heat and beat in the cream. May be served hot or cold. Place a piece of pound cake on each of four plates. Top each with a scoop of ice cream and pour sauce over. *Serves 4.*

CASSEROLE
DINNER V (Using leftover pork)
For Four **Pork and Rice Casserole**
Italian Green Beans
Blueberries and Cream
Coffee   **Milk**

Market List 1 can condensed tomato soup
2 packages frozen Italian green beans
1 quart blueberries
½ pint cream

Check These Cooked pork (2 cups cubed)
Staples Rice (2 cups cooked or ⅔ cup converted)
Thyme
Pepper
Leftover pork gravy (1 cup, or 1 cup beef bouillon)
Prepared stuffing mix (1⅓ cups)
Butter
Superfine sugar

Utensils Measuring cups
Needed Can opener
Measuring spoons
Bowl for mixing stuffing mix

Casserole
Saucepan for cooking beans
Collander
Bowl for blueberries

TIMING   *If dinner is to be served at 7*
If you have to cook the rice:

6:00   Cook rice according to package directions.
If you have leftover rice:

6:24   Preheat oven to 375 degrees.

6:25   Put casserole together.

6:35   Put casserole into oven.

6:40   Prepare blueberries.

6:50   Cook beans according to package directions. Drain and put into saucepan with butter (see recipe).
Serve dinner.
When first course is finished, serve blueberries and cream.

**PORK
AND RICE
CASSEROLE**   This casserole is premised on your having leftover cooked pork in the refrigerator. If you have enough leftover cooked rice also, by any happy chance, you have only the mixing and seasoning of your casserole to do.

2 cups cubed cooked pork
2 cups cooked rice *or* ⅔ cup converted rice, cooked according to package directions

1 can condensed tomato soup
½ teaspoon thyme
Dash pepper
1 cup leftover pork gravy *or* 1 cup beef
 bouillon
1⅓ cups prepared stuffing mix
¼ cup hot water
2 tablespons melted butter

If rice must be cooked for the dish, do that first. Mix pork, rice, soup, thyme, pepper, and gravy or bouillon in a casserole. Mix stuffing mix with water and butter and spread on top. Bake in 375 degree oven until brown on top (20–25 minutes). *Serves 4.*

ITALIAN GREEN BEANS

2 packages frozen Italian green beans
Butter

Cook beans according to package directions. When drained, put back into the pot in which they were cooked with a good hunk of butter and sizzle briefly before serving. *Serves 4–6.*

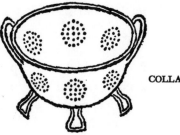

COLLANDER

**BLUEBERRIES
AND CREAM**   1 quart blueberries
½ pint cream
Superfine sugar, if desired

Pick over the blueberries carefully and remove all stems and any traces of leaves which may be present. Put into a collander and hold under running cold water to wash. Drain thoroughly. Place in a bowl and refrigerate until ready to serve with cream and sugar. *Serves 4.*

French Dinner

Just for fun I've given the dishes in this menu for a French dinner in French, with English subtitles. This is partly because many of you may be studying French as your second language—and what a pretty one it is! French food is also pretty and delectable and is the base of a great deal of the world's best cooking, so I'm sure you will enjoy preparing this dinner.

MENU
For Four

Vol-au-Vent de Volaille à la Roi
Chicken à la King in Patty Shells

Petits Pois Bonne Femme
Peas as Cooked by a Good Woman

Pommes de Terre Allumettes
Matchstick Potatoes

Fondue au Chocolat
Chocolate Fondue

Café *Coffee*   **Lait** *Milk*

Market List
1 12-ounce can boned chicken
½ pint light cream
1 4-ounce can sliced mushrooms
1 package frozen patty shells
1 package frozen tiny peas
1 8-ounce can or jar little onions
1 1¾-ounce can potato sticks
Whatever you decide to have for dippers

Check These
Staples
Butter
Flour
Chicken stock base
Salt
Pepper
Pimientos (2)
Lettuce (1 leaf)
Semisweet chocolate (8 squares—1 package)
Milk
Sugar
Cinnamon

Utensils
Needed
Saucepan for chicken in sauce
Measuring cup
Measuring spoons
Mixing spoons
Cookie sheet for heating or baking patty shells
Saucepan for peas
Strainer
Pan for heating potatoes
Saucepan for fondue
Fondue pot or small chafing dish

TIMING *If dinner is to be served at 7*
6:00 Make chicken à la king and keep warm.
6:10 Preheat oven to 450 degrees.
6:20 Put patty shells into oven and turn it down
to 400 degrees.

6:30 Cook peas, drain, mix with butter and onions and keep hot.

6:45 Remove patty shells from oven and place
on a rack.

6:46 Turn oven down to 200 degrees.

6:50 Put potatoes in oven.

6:51 Make chocolate fondue.

**VOL-AU-VENT
DE VOLAILLE
À LA ROI
Chicken
a la King in
Patty Shells**

2 cups cooked or canned chicken, cut up
coarsely

4 tablespoons butter

4 tablespoons flour

1 cup chicken stock (make with a cube or
powdered stock base)

1 cup (½ pint) light cream

Salt and pepper to taste

2 pimientos, cut up coarsely

1 4-ounce can sliced mushrooms, drained.

4 patty shells

Melt butter. Stir in flour thoroughly and cook over low heat
for about a minute, stirring constantly. Add stock and cream
and cook, stirring constantly until thickened. Season to taste
with salt and pepper. Add chicken, pimientos and mushrooms and keep warm over hot water. Serve in patty shells.
Serves four.
Note: Bake frozen patty shells according to package directions. (Put the ones you're not going to use, well wrapped,
back in the freezer.) When they are done, remove each little
center piece, which comes out easily if aided by the point

of a knife. After filling with the chicken, place the little piece of pastry, thus removed, on top.

PETITS POIS
BONNE
FEMME
Peas as
Cooked by a
Good Woman

1 package frozen tiny peas
1 large lettuce leaf
1 8-ounce can or jar little onions, drained
2 tablespoons butter

Cook the peas according to package directions, adding the lettuce leaf. When done, drain and remove lettuce leaf. Melt the butter in the same pot. Add drained onions and peas and warm well over low heat, stirring occasionally. Serves 4.

POMMES
DE TERRE
ALLUMETTES
Matchstick
Potatoes

1 1¾-ounce can potato sticks
1 tablespoon butter
Dash of salt

Place potato sticks in an ovenproof pan. Dot with butter and sprinkle with salt. Heat well for about 10 minutes in a 200 degree oven. *Serves 4.*

FONDUE AU
CHOCOLAT
Chocolate
Fondue

8 squares semisweet chocolate
½ cup, plus 1 tablespoon, milk
¼ cup sugar
Dash cinnamon
Dippers (see below)

Combine chocolate, milk, sugar, and cinnamon in a sauce-pan. Place over low heat and stir occasionally until chocolate is melted and mixture is perfectly smooth. Pour into a fondue pot or small chafing dish. Keep warm while serving. Arrange dippers on a tray or platter beside fondue. Let each person dip his favorites into the chocolate. If fondue is kept warm more than 30 minutes, add more milk as needed to maintain proper consistency. For individual servings ladle fondue into demitasse cups or small glasses and serve immediately. Makes about 1½ cups.

FONDUE POT

Possible Dippers   *Choose two or three of your favorites*
Seedless green grapes
Apples slices or wedges

Possible
Dippers
(cont.)
Banana chunks or slices
Pear wedges
Stemmed cherries
Tangerine sections
Dried apricots
Prunes
Dates
Candied orange rind
Butter cookies
Toasted pound cake strips
Pretzels
Rolled cookies
Ladyfingers
Flat mints

Italian Dinner

The favorite foreign food of most Americans is Italian, so you must certainly round out your ability to present a foreign dinner party for family or friends with typical food of that country. It's easy to make and to serve—and delicious.

MENU
For Six

Spaghetti with Meat Sauce

Green Salad

Hot Italian Bread

Spumoni

Coffee   Milk

Market List

1 pound chopped beef
1 15-ounce can Italian tomato purée
½ pound Parmesan cheese
Small bunch of parsley
1 pound spaghetti
1 head escarole
1 head Boston lettuce
1 large round loaf Italian bread
6 cups spumoni (or 1 quart ice cream)

Check These Staples
Onions, or frozen, chopped onions (2 cups, chopped)
Garlic
Olive oil
Stewed or canned tomatoes (2 cups)
Honey
Bouillon cube or powdered beef stock
Salt and pepper
Vinegar

Utensils Needed
Large saucepan or Dutch oven for meat sauce
Measuring cup
Cheese grater
Fork
Saucepan for cooking spaghetti
Strainer
Clean tea towel
Bowl for mixing salad dressing
Cookie sheet for heating bread

TIMING *If dinner is to be served at 7*

4:45 Make meat sauce. Check occasionally to see whether it needs more beef stock.

6:00 Wash greens, shake to remove excess moisture, wrap in clean tea towel and refrigerate to crisp.

6:35 Put salad together.

6:40 Preheat oven to 375 degrees.

6:45 Bring water for spaghetti to the boil.

6:47 Cook spaghetti.

6:50 Put bread into oven to heat.

6:56 Drain spaghetti.
Serve dinner.
When first course is finished, serve the spumoni or ice cream.

SPAGHETTI WITH MEAT SAUCE

2 cups chopped onion
1 clove garlic, mashed
¼ cup olive oil
1 pound chopped beef
1 cup Italian tomato purée
2 cups stewed (or canned) tomatoes
1 teaspoon honey
½ cup beef stock
1 teaspoon salt
Pepper to taste
½ cup grated Parmesan cheese
2 tablespoons chopped fresh parsley
Big dish of grated Parmesan cheese
1 pound spaghetti

Sauté onions and garlic in oil until lightly browned. Add meat and cook, stirring constantly with a fork, until it loses its red color. Add tomato purée, tomatoes, honey, stock, salt, pepper, and the ½ cup of grated Parmesan. Simmer gently 2 hours, adding more beef stock if necessary, but the sauce should be thick. Cook spaghetti in boiling, salted water, with a dash of olive oil in it (to keep it from sticking together) for 9 minutes. It will be *al dente*—not soft, but so that you know you're biting on it. Drain well. Serve with the meat sauce poured over, the parsley sprinkled on and plenty of grated Parmesan in a separate dish to sprinkle on top. *Serves 6.*
Note: The sauce can be made anytime, refrigerated and reheated.

GREEN
SALAD
1 head escarole
1 head Boston lettuce
French dressing (see page 200)

Wash greens well ahead of time, shake to remove excess moisture, wrap in a clean tea towel, and refrigerate to crisp. When ready to serve, tear the greens in bite-size pieces into a salad bowl. Pour French dressing over the greens. Toss well to coat all leaves. *Serves 6.*

HOT
ITALIAN
BREAD
1 large round loaf Italian bread

Place the bread on a cookie sheet and put into a 375 degree oven for 10 minutes. Serve with plenty of butter available.

SPUMONI

Many freezer cases have Italian spumoni in them, but if you can't find it, your favorite ice cream will do very well and be quite authentic, as the Italians make the world's best ice cream. If you have an Italian market near you, perhaps you can add the extra touch of those lovely macaroons they sell in gay tissue paper wrappings.

A Mexican Party

One of the easiest national parties to prepare for your friends is a Mexican one, as you will see from the suggested menu offered here. The possible decorations are fun, too. Start with the colors of the Mexican flag—red, white, green, and a golden yellow. What a gay table their use can make! Start, for instance, with a white tablecloth. Use red paper napkins, green leaves, and yellow straw flowers, or any fresh yellow flower that's in season, and you've involved all those gay flag colors already. Further decorations could include sombreros so typical of our neighbor south of the border. Perhaps you'd like to make place cards in this shape and color them brilliantly. If your family owns any Mexican pottery, be sure to put it into use, at least for the centerpiece—and perhaps for serving dishes as well.

MENU
For Six

Chili Con Carne

Tortillas

Grapefruit and Avocado Salad

Flan

Coffee   Milk

Market List
1 11-ounce can tortillas or 1 9-ounce package frozen
2 1-pound cans chili con carne with beans
½ pound ground chuck
2 grapefruit
1 ripe avocado
1 medium-sized head Boston lettuce

Check These Staples
Sugar (1 cup)
Eggs (4)
Salt
Milk (3 cups)
Vanilla
Onions (1 small or 2 tablespoons dehydrated minced, reconstituted)
Bacon fat
Chili powder
Olive oil
Vinegar or lemon juice
Pepper

Utensils Needed
Small heavy skillet
Wooden spoon
6 custard cups
Double boiler
Bowl for mixing custard
Spoon for beating and mixing
Flat knife
Napkin or cloth
Measuring cups
Measuring spoons
Aluminum foil
Skillet for browning onions
Saucepan for chili con carne
Grapefruit knife or paring knife
Glass for juice
Salad bowl
Paring knife
Clean tea towel
Small bowl for mixing dressing
Custard cups
Shallow pan for hot water

TIMING   *If dinner is to be served at 7*

At least four hours before the party, make the flan, or, if you prefer, the night before (in which case cover the custards with foil or plastic wrap for refrigerating).

5:45   Prepare lettuce and refrigerate it.

6:00   Preheat oven to 200 degrees (if using canned tortillas).

6:01   Prepare tortillas for heating.

6:10   Place tortillas in oven.

6:15   Prepare chili con carne and keep warm, covered (over a pan of hot water or transfer to a double boiler).

6:30   Prepare salad. Cover with plastic wrap and toss just before serving.

6:35   Place frozen tortillas in boiling water as instructed on the package, if you're using them.

Serve the dinner.

When the first course is finished, unmold and serve the flan.

FLAN   1 cup granulated sugar
4 eggs
¼ teaspoon salt
3 cups scalded milk (see page 11)
1 teaspoon vanilla

In a small, heavy skillet heat ½ *cup* of the sugar, stirring constantly with a wooden spoon until the sugar melts and turns caramel color, being very careful not to let it burn. Pour into each of six custard cups. Beat eggs slightly in a bowl. Add remaining sugar and salt and pour the milk on slowly, stirring to blend. Add vanilla. Pour gently into the custard cups so that the caramel will remain in the bottom. Place cups in a shallow pan of hot water and bake in 350 degree oven until a knife inserted in the middle of a flan comes out clean (about 30 minutes). Cool at room temperature. Chill in the refrigerator. When ready to serve, run the blunt tip of a flat knife between the cup and the flan. Turn out into individual serving dishes. *Serves 6.*

TORTILLAS   1 11-ounce can tortillas or
                 1 9-ounce bag frozen tortillas

If you use the canned variety, open the can at both ends and push the tortillas out. There are about 18 in an 11-ounce can. If you do not wish to use them all, wrap as many as you're going to keep in waxed paper, leaving in the papers which come between them in the can, and store in the refrigerator for future use. Wrap the ones you're going to use for this party in a damp cloth or napkin, then in aluminum foil, and place in a 200 degree oven to warm. Serve as bread with the chili con carne.

If you use frozen tortillas you will find that the package contains 12 of them. Heat in the bag in boiling water according to package directions.

CHILI
CON CARNE   2 1-pound cans chili con carne with beans
               2 tablespoons minced onion
               1 tablespoon bacon fat
               ½ pound ground chuck
               2 teaspoons chili powder (or to taste)

In a skillet fry the onion in the bacon fat until golden brown. Add beef and cook, breaking up with a fork constantly, until meat loses its red color. Add to chili con carne in a saucepan. Add chili powder and mix well. Heat thoroughly. *Serves 6.* **Note:** Most Americans don't like very hotly seasoned food, though Mexicans love it dearly. Thus, the chili con carne you buy in cans is very lightly seasoned by Mexican standards, and I recommend adding at least a bit more of the chili powder which is supposed to flavor it. Do this, as usual in seasoning, very lightly, taste and add more if you think your friends can take it and still keep their cool.

GRAPEFRUIT
AND
AVOCADO
SALAD　　2 grapefruit
　　　　　　　1 ripe avocado
　　　　　　　1 medium-sized head Boston lettuce
　　　　　　　French dressing (see page 200)

Any time before you actually start preparing the party, wash the lettuce, shake to remove excess water, and wrap in a clean tea towel. Refrigerate to crisp. Cut grapefruit in half crosswise and remove seeds. With a grapefruit knife, carefully lift out the segments into a salad bowl. Squeeze the juice from the shells into a glass. When all segments are removed, pour the juice which will have collected around them into the same glass. There should be a nice glassful for somebody's breakfast next morning. When ready to put the salad together, peel the avocado and remove the pit. Cut into thin slices and add to grapefruit in the salad bowl. Tear the lettuce into the bowl. Add French dressing and toss gently to mix, being careful not to break up the avocado. *Serves 6.*

Scandinavian
Smörgåsbord

A Scandinavian Smörgåsbord offers one of the easiest ways to entertain deliciously. Guests serve themselves, as at any buffet arrangement. You must have a lot of plates, so that clean ones can be used for each foray on the smörgåsbord table. Paper ones will do very well and save a lot of washing up. Every bit of food is placed on the table before the party begins. You must have some sort of arrangement for keeping the hot foods hot—a hot tray, chafing dishes, candle warmers—whatever's available. The various kinds of fish which are eaten at the start are quite correctly served in their open tins. Provide little lemon or pickle forks or toothpicks to remove the fish from the tins, plus a couple of spoons so that anyone who wants more sauce can easily get it. Next, the hot foods are eaten. The windup is salad and cheese. The breads are, of course, eaten with each of the courses, as are the condiments. The menu below is about as simple as it can be. You may add to it if you wish, but it seems wiser not to try too much the first time. You can, for instance, have several types of herring. You might add jars of the delicious little Danish shrimp. You can also have a variety of salads if you like. If you are lucky enough to live where there is a Scandinavian food shop, you have only to explore it to find an almost bewildering array of treats.

MENU
For Twelve

Fillets of Herring   Sardines
Rolled Anchovies
Carrot and Celery Sticks
Stuffed Olives
Watermelon Pickles
Breads
Butter
Swedish Meat Balls
Brown Bean Casserole
Green Salad
Assorted Cheeses
Coffee   Milk

Market List

Herring fillets (3–4 tins)
Sardines (2–3 tins)
Bunch of celery
Bunch of carrots
1½ pounds ground beef
½ pound ground veal
½ pound ground pork
3 1-pound cans kidney beans
1 head Boston lettuce ⎱ or others
1 bunch watercress ⎰ of your
1 head romaine ⎰ choice
Cheeses of your choice—you will need about
2 pounds of at least 2 kinds

Check These Staples

Eggs (2)
Milk (1 cup for cooking)
White bread (for making soft crumbs)
Butter (at least 3 sticks)
Onion (½ cup, minced)
Salt
Pepper
Nutmeg
Allspice
Olive oil
Vinegar
Lemons
Large jar stuffed olives
Jar of watermelon pickle
1 loaf soft rye bread
1 box Finn Crisp
1 loaf dark pumpernickel

Utensils Needed

Can opener
Measuring cup
Bowl for crisping vegetable sticks
Sharp knife
Clean tea towel
Bowl for mixing meat balls
Large skillet
Casserole for meat balls
Casserole for kidney beans
Salad bowl
Bowl for mixing French dressing
Board to serve cheeses on

TIMING

If Smörgåsbord is to be served at 7

5:00 Make carrot and celery sticks. Refrigerate.
5:25 Wash greens, shake to remove excess water, wrap in a clean tea towel. Place in refrigerator to crisp.
5:30 Make meatballs.
5:50 Refrigerate meatballs.

5:55   Place beans in casserole.

6:00   Open cans or jars of fish and place on serving trays.

6:05   Put olives and pickles into serving dishes.

6:10   Place breads in basket or other container.

6:20   Preheat oven to 350 degrees.

6:21   Fry meatballs.

(If meatballs were made the night before, take them from the refrigerator at 6 and place them in the oven at 6:30.)

6:35   Place beans in oven.

6:45   Tear greens into salad bowl and toss with French dressing.

6:55   Drain carrot and celery sticks and place in serving dish.

7:00   Serve the dinner.

FILLETS OF HERRING

Fillets of herring come in a great variety of sauces—dill, wine, mustard, etc. The tins are quite small (so are the herring) so you will need several for twelve people. You can buy all the same kind or vary them, which is more fun. You can also add herring in sour cream, which you would buy in a delicatessen.

SARDINES

Sardines also come in sauces, but I think just plain boneless and skinless Norwegian ones are best for this party. The herring will provide enough sauces. Have wedges of lemon available for those who like to spark either sardines or, if you add them to the menu, the tiny shrimp.

CARROT AND
CELERY
STICKS
8 carrots
6 stalks of celery

Wash and scrape carrots. Wash celery. With a sharp knife cut carrots and celery into pieces about 3 inches long and ¼ inch wide. Place in a bowl of cold water and refrigerate until serving time. *Enough for 12.*

BREADS

A variety of breads is always offered at a Smörgåsbord. I would suggest that you provide a soft rye bread, Finn Crisp, and a dark pumpernickel. A basket makes an attractive holder for them.

SWEDISH
MEATBALLS
1½ pounds ground beef
½ pound ground veal
½ pound ground pork
2 eggs
1 cup milk
3 cups soft breadcrumbs
½ cup (1 stick) butter
¼ cup minced onion
1 tablespoon salt
¼ teaspoon pepper
½ teaspoon nutmeg
½ teaspoon allspice

Have the meats ground twice by the butcher. In a large bowl combine egg, milk, and breadcrumbs. Let stand 10 minutes.

In a large skillet, melt 2 tablespoons of the butter and sauté onion over low heat until tender. Add, with meat and seasonings, to breadcrumb mixture and mix thoroughly. Shape into 1-inch balls. Chill for at least ½ hour. Melt remaining butter in same skillet and brown a few meatballs at a time, shaking pan frequently to keep the balls round. Place in a covered casserole. If to be served almost at once, keep warm in a 350 degree oven. If you wish to make the meatballs the night before the party, store the casserole in the refrigerator. Remove from refrigerator and let stand at room temperature for 30 minutes. Then heat in 350 degee oven 20 to 30 minutes. *Makes 12 servings of about 5 meatballs each.*

BROWN BEAN CASSEROLE   3 1-pound cans kidney beans

Pour beans, with their liquid, into a casserole. Cover and warm through in a 350 degree oven (about 25 minutes). *Serves 12.*

Note: The Swedes make a brown bean casserole from scratch, which is delicious and something of a bother. It seems to me more sensible for you to use the canned variety—and kidney beans taste especially good with Swedish meatballs.

GREEN SALAD

You will know by now that a green salad can consist of almost any combination of greens you care to use, or of just one green tossed with French dressing (see page 200). Here are some of the greens you might like to try for variety, texture, and flavor: Iceberg, Boston, or Bibb (limestone) lettuce, romaine, chickory, escarole, endive—Belgian or domestic—spinach, water cress, or dandelion greens.

ASSORTED
CHEESES

If you live where there is a Scandinavian food shop, you can have a grand time looking over the great variety of cheeses to be had and deciding which you will serve. For a party of 12 buy at least two kinds. One great favorite in Norway is Gjetost, which is a sort of chocolate brown color and, for my taste, a rather unappetizing flavor, but Norwegians love it and maybe you would too! Then, there are many Scandinavian cheeses flavored with caraway or cumin seed. They, in my opinion, are delicious and if you can't find one, buy Muenster flavored with caraway seed, as it is readily available all over the United States. Danish blue is a lovely cheese and makes a good contrast to a caraway cheese, for instance. Remove from the refrigerator a couple of hours before the party. Cheese which has been brought to room temperature improves greatly in flavor.

A Valentine's Day Party

This would probably be a party a girl would give for her friends, perhaps as a Saturday luncheon "do." Make it as pink-and-red-and-white as possible, with decorations to carry out the theme—all hearts and flowers. Red hearts and pink candles look nifty together. A Valentine-printed paper tablecloth would be nice with either red or white napkins to set it off. Have little pink ruffled cups at each place, decorated with red paper hearts and filled with heart-shaped candies.

MENU
For Six

Cream of Tomato Soup
American Cheese Fondue
Beet and Onion Salad
Strawberry Bavarian
Heart-shaped Cookies
Coffee   Milk

Market List
1 package strawberry-flavor gelatin
1 envelope whipped topping mix or ½ pint whipping cream
Frozen or fresh strawberries
Decorations of your choice for cookies
½ pound Cheddar cheese
1 1-pound, 4-ounce can sliced beets
1 Bermuda onion
2 heads Bibb lettuce or 1 head Boston lettuce
2 cans (10½ ounces) condensed tomato soup

Check These Staples
Sugar
Flour
Baking powder
Salt
Butter (½ cup, plus)
Eggs (4)
Vanilla
Milk (1½ cups, plus)
Bread (2 cups soft crumbs)
Cayenne
Pimientos (2)
1 pint half-and-half
½ pint heavy cream
Olive oil
Vinegar
Pepper

Utensils Needed
Bowl for gelatin
Bowl for whipping topping mix or cream
Electric or rotary beater
1-quart mold
Measuring cup
Measuring spoons
Flour sifter
Bowl for flour mixture
Bowl for butter mixture
Rolling pin
Pastry cloth and sleeve
Cookie cutter (heart-shaped)
Baking sheet or sheets

Bowl for breadcrumbs
Bowl for egg yolks
Bowl for egg whites
Mixing spoons
Baking dish
Clean tea cloth
Strainer
Paring knife
Bowl for salad dressing
Saucepan for soup
Bowl for whipping cream

TIMING   *If luncheon is to be at 1* P.M.

Early in the morning (about 8 o'clock) make Strawberry Bavarian.

Immediately make cookies.

11:30	Put crumbs to soak in milk for fondue.
11:45	Wash, shake to remove excess moisture, and refrigerate lettuce in clean tea towel.
12:00	Finish preparing fondue.
12:05	Preheat oven to 350 degrees.
12:15	Place fondue in oven.
12:30	Prepare salad.
12:45	Put soup on to heat.
12:50	Whip cream for soup.
1:00	Serve luncheon.

After soup and main course are finished, serve dessert.

STRAWBERRY BAVARIAN

1 package strawberry-flavored gelatin
¼ cup sugar
1 cup boiling water

¾ cup cold water
1 envelope whipped topping mix or
1 cup whipping cream

Dissolve gelatin and sugar in boiling water. Add cold water. Chill until slightly thickened. Prepare topping mix as directed on package or whip the cream (see page 201). Stir 1½ cups into gelatin until blended. Pour into a 1-quart mold (heart-shaped, preferably). Chill until firm (about four hours). Unmold (see page 13) and serve surrounded by defrosted frozen strawberries or fresh whole strawberries and remaining topping or cream. *Serves 6.*

HEART-SHAPED AND
1-QUART RING MOLD

**HEART-
SHAPED
COOKIES**   1 recipe sugar cookies (see page 201)

Decorate with pink and red gumdrops, candy hearts, silver and pink sprinkles—what you will—or with pink or red icing (see page 203) if you prefer.

AMERICAN
CHEESE
FONDUE

1½ cups milk
2 cups soft breadcrumbs
1½ cups grated Cheddar cheese
1 teaspoon salt
Dash cayenne
2 tablespoons melted butter
3 egg yolks, well beaten
3 egg whites, beaten stiff (see page 7)

Pour milk over breadcrumbs and let stand at least 30 minutes. Add cheese, seasonings, butter, and egg yolks, and mix well. Fold in egg whites. Turn into a buttered baking dish and bake in 350 degree oven until puffed and browned (about 45 minutes). *Serves 6.*

BEET AND
ONION
SALAD

1 1-pound, 4-ounce can sliced beets
1 Bermuda onion
2 heads Bibb lettuce or 1 head Boston lettuce
2 pimientos, cut in thin strips
6 tablespoons olive oil
2 tablespoons vinegar
Salt and pepper to taste

Wash lettuce, shake to remove excess moisture, wrap in a clean tea cloth and refrigerate to crisp. Drain the beets thoroughly. Place lettuce on 6 salad plates. Place beets on top. Peel the onion, slice it thinly, and place slices over beets. Decorate each salad with pimiento strips. Mix olive oil, vinegar, salt and pepper. Pour over salads. *Serves 6.*

CREAM OF TOMATO SOUP

2 cans (10½ ounces) condensed tomato soup

1½ cans half-and-half (use soup can as measure)

½ cup heavy cream

Dash salt

Mix soup with half-and-half, stirring to blend well. Heat, but do not boil. Whip cream with salt until thick (see page 201). When serving, top each cup or soup plate with a dollop of whipped cream. *Serves 6.*

St. Patrick's Day Dinner

It's always fun to plan a menu emphasizing one color, and St. Patrick's Day offers a lovely opportunity for just that. Never, by any chance, plan a meal which is literally all one color. Nothing could be duller, especially if it's all white (what the French call a *menu blanc*, which they rarely present). When you plan a St. Patrick's Day dinner, it's easy to provide color and atmosphere in your decorations. For instance you might have an emerald-green paper tablecloth and napkins and set a little pot of shamrocks in front of each guest as a favor to be taken home. Here's a menu with enough green concomitants to be timely, but also with enough variety and contrast to be delicious.

MENU Pea Soup
For Six Roast Leg of Lamb
Mint Jelly
Potatoes Colcannon
Green Bean Casserole
Pistachio Ice Cream   Shamrock Cookies
Green and White Mints
Coffee   Milk

Market List	1 5-pound leg of lamb
	1 jar mint jelly
	6 baking potatoes
	Small head of cabbage (or 2 cups leftover, cooked)
	Frenched green beans
	1 3½-ounce can French fried onions
	Fresh parsley
	2 cans condensed pea soup
	1 quart pistachio ice cream
Check These Staples	If you're going to make the cookies:
	Butter (1 stick)
	Sugar
	Eggs (1)
	Milk
	Vanilla
	Salt
	Baking powder
	Flour
	Otherwise add cookies to your market list and check only:
	Salt
	Pepper
	Butter (½ sitck)
	1 can condensed mushroom soup
	Soy sauce
Utensils Needed	**For cookies:**
	Bowl for mixing cookies
	Measuring cups
	Measuring spoons
	Flour sifter
	Foil
	Pastry board (preferably with cloth)
	Rolling pin
	Shamrock cutter
	Cookie sheet or sheets
	Spatula
	Wire rack
	For dinner:
	Roasting pan and rack

Meat thermometer
Bowl for mashing and mixing potatoes
Saucepan for green beans
1 quart casserole
Strainer

TIMING *If dinner is to be served at 7*

Early in the day, or the day before, make cookies, unless you're going to buy them.

4:55	Preheat oven to 325 degrees.
5:05	Put roast into oven (for medium lamb).
5:16	Cook cabbage if you have none left over.
5:30	Put potatoes into oven.
6:00	Prepare soup for heating.
6:15	Prepare casserole of beans.
6:30	Place bean casserole in oven.
6:40	Remove lamb from oven.
6:42	Remove potatoes from oven and complete preparation.
6:50	Heat soup.
6:55	Run potatoes under broiler. Keep warm in turned-off oven.
	Serve soup.
	Serve main course.
	Serve dessert.

SHAMROCK COOKIES

The bakeries are full of cookies shaped like shamrocks at this time of the year so if you haven't time to make any you can easily buy some. If you do want to make your own, however, proceed as follows:

½ cup (1 stick) softened butter
1 cup sugar
1 egg
1 tablespoon milk
½ teaspoon vanilla
½ teaspoon salt
1 teaspoon baking powder
1¾ cups flour

Let butter stand at room temperature to soften. Beat in sugar, egg, milk, and vanilla. Mix and sift salt, baking powder, and flour and add to egg mixture, mixing well. Wrap dough in foil and refrigerate for at least an hour. Roll out, ½ at a time, on a floured board or cloth to ¼ inch thickness. Cut with shamrock cookie cutter, dipped into flour. Do the same with remaining dough. Also, pick up the scraps remaining from the cutting and press them together with a light touch. Roll out again and cut more shamrocks. Transfer shamrocks to a greased cookie sheet or sheets with a spatula. Bake in 375 degree oven about 8 minutes. Remove from sheet with spatula and cool on wire rack. Decorate with green sprinkles if you like. *Makes about 4 dozen shamrocks.*

POTATOES
COLCANNON

6 baking potatoes
2 cups boiled cabbage, chopped
¼ cup (½ stick) butter
Salt and pepper

Scrub potatoes and bake in 325 degree oven 1 hour and 20 minutes, or until soft when squeezed with a pot holder to protect your hand. Remove from oven, cut in half lengthwise and remove potato. Mash. Mix with cabbage, butter, and salt and pepper to taste. Refill potato shells. Run under the broiler to brown lightly. *Serves 6.*

MEAT THERMOMETER

ROAST LEG OF LAMB

1 5-pound leg of lamb
Salt and pepper

Sprinkle lamb with salt and pepper. Place on a rack in an open roasting pan and roast in a 325 degree oven 18 minutes a pound for well done (180 degrees on meat thermometer), 15 minutes a pound for medium (165 degrees on meat thermometer), or 12 minutes a pound for rare (140 degrees on meat thermometer). Let roast stand outside the oven for 20 minutes on a hot serving platter before carving to settle the juices. *Serves 6.*

PEA SOUP

2 cans condensed green pea soup

Prepare soup according to directions on can, using either water or milk to dilute it. Decorate with sprigs of parsley. *Serves 6.*

GREEN BEAN
CASSEROLE

2 packages frozen Frenched green beans
1 can condensed mushroom soup
⅓ cup milk
1 teaspoon soy sauce
Dash pepper
1 3½-ounce can French fried onions

Cook the beans according to package directions and drain well. Meantime, pour soup, milk, and soy sauce into a 1-quart casserole. Add pepper and stir until smooth. Mix in drained beans and half of the onions. Bake in 350 degree oven 25 minutes or until hot. Top with remaining onions. Bake 5 minutes longer. *Serves 6.*

Easter Dinner

Ham is traditional for Easter, and usually it consists of a large boiled or baked one, but I think it might be easiest for you to start your career of cooking ham by working out on a ham slice. It provides plenty for four and if you have a much larger company to serve on Easter Day, you can just get two slices and proceed to double the recipe, as well as the rest of those offered, except the caramel ring which is plenty to serve six, or maybe even eight.

Decorate the Easter dinner table with spring flowers, dyed hard-cooked eggs, bunnies, or whatever else seems seasonable to you. It should be light and gay and full of the spirit of joy.

MENU	Hot Bouillon with Avocado Slices
For Four	Pineapple Ham Slice
	Sweet Potatoes with Marshmallows
	Asparagus
	Melba Toast
	Caramel Ring with Ice Cream
	Coffee Milk

Market List 1 1-pound, 2-ounce can sweet potatoes
Marshmallows (you need 8–10)
1 large ham slice, cut 1-inch thick (weight about 1½ lbs.)
1 8½-ounce can crushed pineapple
1 bunch asparagus
2 cans beef bouillon
1 ripe avocado
1 pint ice cream or sherbets

Check These Staples Light brown sugar (1½ cups)
Light corn syrup
½ cup milk
Butter (1 stick, plus 4 tbsp.)
Cornflakes (6 cups)
Milk
Salt

Utensils Needed Saucepan for syrup
Measuring cup
Measuring spoons
Wooden spoon
Mixing bowl
1-quart ring mold
Ice cream scoop
Can opener
Double boiler
Potato masher
Casserole
Skillet for ham
Tongs to turn ham
2 saucepans (one of which can be inverted on top of the other)
Strainer
Vegetable peeler
Soft white string
Fork
Saucepan for soup
Paring knife
Plastic wrap

TIMING   *If dinner is to be served at 7*

As early in the morning as possible, make the caramel ring.

5:45   Prepare sweet potato casserole.

6:10   Prepare asparagus and tie with string.

6:29   Preheat oven to 400 degrees.

6:30   Prepare ham slice. Keep warm until ready to serve.

6:40   Put potatoes into oven. When marshmallows are brown, turn off oven and leave the potatoes in it until ready to serve.

6:43   Cook asparagus. Drain when done to your taste.

6:45   Put soup on to heat.

6:50   Slice avocado.

Serve the soup.

Serve the main course.

Serve the Caramel Ring.

CARAMEL RING   1½ cups light brown sugar
2 tablespoons light corn syrup
½ cup milk
¼ cup (½ stick) butter
6 cups cornflakes

In a saucepan combine sugar, syrup, milk, and butter. Bring to the boil and boil until it reaches the soft ball stage, about 20 minutes (240 degrees on the candy thermometer). Meantime, butter a 1-quart ring mold with a large hole in the center. Put cornflakes into a large bowl. When syrup is ready, pour it over the cornflakes and mix well with a wooden spoon. Press mixture into the ring mold. Cover with plastic wrap and let stand at room temperature for 6–8 hours. When ready to serve, unmold (it comes out very easily) and fill the center of the ring with balls of ice cream (strawberry would be pretty) or with balls of sherbet in various pastel colors. *Serves 6–8.*

Note: The ring becomes very crisp, so it is impossible to slice it to serve. You just have to break it up, as it crumbles easily. It is absolutely delicious.

SWEET POTATOES WITH MARSHMALLOWS

1 1-pound, 2-ounce can sweet potatoes
Milk
2 tablespoons butter
8–10 marshmallows

Remove potatoes from can and heat in the top of a double boiler over hot water. Mash them, beating in enough milk to make them fluffy. Beat in the butter. Place in a casserole and dot the top with marshmallows. Bake in 400 degree oven until marshmallows are melted and lightly brown (about 20 minutes).

ASPARAGUS

1 bunch asparagus
1 teaspoon salt
½ cup melted butter

Wash asparagus and cut off "woody" bottoms of stalks. With

a vegetable peeler peel each stalk from below the green tips to the bottom. Tie all together with soft white string. Bring water to boil in a saucepan. Add salt. Stand the asparagus in the water so that the tips are exposed just above the surface. Cover the pan with another saucepan, inverted over it (the lid almost certainly won't fit over the standing asparagus). Boil until done to your taste, 12 to 15 minutes. Test by poking the bottom part of the stalks with a fork. Drain well and serve doused in melted butter. *Serves 4.*

Note: If you prefer, you may cook frozen asparagus tips according to package directions and serve them in the same way.

TONGS

**PINEAPPLE
HAM SLICE**

1 ham slice, cut 1-inch thick
2 tablespoons butter
1 8½-ounce can crushed pineapple

Make gashes in the fat around the edge of the ham (so it won't curl when being browned). Melt butter in a skillet and brown the ham on both sides. Pour in pineapple, lower heat, and simmer, covered, for 20 minutes. Serve on hot platter with pineapple poured over. *Serves 4–6.*

HOT BOUILLON WITH AVOCADO SLICES

2 cans beef bouillon
1 can water
8 slices ripe avocado

Heat bouillon and water to piping. Serve with two slices of avocado floating on top of each cup or bowl. Peel the avocado and remove the pit. Slice the avocado at the last minute so it won't discolor. If there is some left over, wrap it closely in plastic wrap and it will hold its color quite well. *Serves 4.*

Mother's Day Breakfast

One of the big objects of celebrating Mother's Day is to make your mother feel pampered and taken care of for the entire day, if possible. Perhaps the best thing you can do for her is to give her breakfast in bed, which is a rare treat for most busy housekeepers and working women. Be sure that the breakfast tray is attractive and neat. It should be set with a place mat and matching napkin—of paper if you like. There should be a flower in a bud vase, even if it's an artificial one. The cream should be in a little pitcher, the marmalade in a little jam jar. There should be a cover for the plate which contains the entree so that it may keep warm. If the house contains no such thing, improvise with heavy duty foil. Coffee should be in one well-heated pot and hot milk in another (see recipe).

MENU	Strawberries and Cream
	Toad-in-the-Hole
	Hot Croissants Marmalade
	Café au Lait

Market List	1 pint box of strawberries Croissants from the bakery or in a package
Check These Staples	Superfine sugar Cream Bread (one slice) Egg (one) Butter Salt and pepper Marmalade Milk
Utensils Needed	Measuring cup Strainer Pan for heating croissants Small saucepan for heating milk 2½-inch cookie cutter 8-inch skillet Measuring spoons Cup into which to break egg Pancake turner Paring knife or huller

TIMING *If breakfast is to be served at 9*

Let her sleep until whatever is late for *her!*

8:30 Prepare strawberries and refrigerate.

8:40 Preheat oven to 400 degrees.

8:45 Prepare bread for toad-in-the-hole.

8:50 Put croissants into oven.

8:51 Make toad-in-the-hole.

8:55 Put on milk to heat for café au lait.

Serve on your beautiful breakfast tray.

STRAWBERRIES
AND CREAM

1 cup strawberries
Superfine sugar, if desired
Small pitcher of cream

Wash the strawberries in a sieve under gently running cold water. Drain well. Remove hulls either with your fingers or with the help of a paring knife or, best of all, with a little metal huller which can be found in any housewares store. Serve in a pretty glass bowl or one which matches the china you're using on the tray. Sprinkle with a little superfine sugar if your mother likes that and refrigerate until you set up the tray. The cream goes on the tray with the bowl of berries.

HOT
CROISSANTS

You can buy croissants from a bakery or in a package at the supermarket. Heat in 400 degree oven until piping (about 10 minutes). Serve on a butter plate with a good pat of butter.

CAFÉ
AU LAIT

Nowhere in this book have I told you how to make coffee because I take for granted that your family has a favorite method, whether it be just hot water and instant coffee, drip, percolator, or any other. Just be sure that you put hot water into the pot to warm it before you fill it and that the coffee is hot. The same goes for the pot in which you serve the hot milk, which should be heated but not boiled. When your mother is ready to drink it she will pour from both pots at once an equal quantity of hot milk and coffee, which is how the French make café au lait.

TOAD-IN-THE-HOLE

1 slice white bread
3 tablespoons butter
1 egg
Salt and pepper

Leave the crust on the bread to help hold the shape of the hole. Cut a round piece from the center of the bread with a 2½-inch cookie cutter. Melt half the butter in an 8-inch skillet and put in the bread slice. Break the egg into a cup and slide it carefully into the hole in the bread. Season to taste with salt and pepper. Cook over medium heat until the egg is set and the bread nicely browned on the bottom. Add the remaining butter. Carefully slide a pancake turner under the whole toad-in-the-hole and turn it over. Brown the second side. Serve on a plate, covered, so it will keep warm while your mother enjoys her strawberries first.

Note: The skillet should be at least an 8-inch one so you can slide the pancake turner in easily.

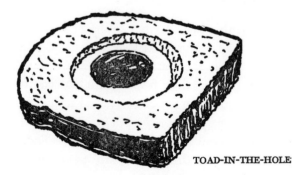

TOAD-IN-THE-HOLE

Father's Day Dinner

Since most fathers aren't the family cooks, if you give a dinner party for yours on Father's Day, it is largely to show him how much you love him and not (as you do for Mother on her Day) to save him work! Try to plan a meal which will include his favorite foods—and, especially if he's a great outdoor cook, not the sort of food he already cooks superbly himself! I think most men will like the Party Beef Stew suggested below; in fact I'm sure of it from having served it to so many. It makes an easy meal to prepare because all the vegetables are right in it. All you need to provide in addition is bread and potatoes. Furthermore, this stew is even better if it's made the day before and reheated, so perhaps you'd like to do it that way.

MENU   **Party Beef Stew**
For Six   **Potatoes au Gratin**
        Garlic French Bread
        Apple Crunch
        Coffee   **Milk**

Market List
2 pounds rump of beef, cut in 1-inch cubes
4 medium onions
1 large bunch carrots
1 1-pound, 13-ounce can tomatoes
2 packages frozen Frenched green beans
1 1-pound can kidney beans
½ pint sour cream
Brown-and-serve French bread
3 pounds cooking apples

Check These Staples
Salt
Pepper
Butter (1½ sticks plus 2 tablespoons)
Paprika
Beef bouillon cubes or powdered beef stock
Chili powder
Cornstarch
Mashed potato mix
Cheddar cheese (¼ pound)
Garlic or garlic powder
Flour
Sugar
Nutmeg

Utensils Needed
Dutch oven (or other large pot with lid)
Measuring cup
Measuring spoons
Can opener
Bowl for blending cornstarch
Mixing spoon
Saucepan for making mashed potatoes
Casserole for potatoes
Cheese grater
Bowl for making garlic butter
Flat knife
Cookie sheet for baking bread
Paring knife
Apple corer
Baking dish
Bowl for making paste for crunch

TIMING   *If dinner is to be served at 7*

About 3 hours time is required for making the stew (during part of that time you will be just waiting for the meat to cook). So if you make it the day before, just allow the same amount of time. The day of the party, take stew from the refrigerator an hour before dinner and reheat over low heat. If you make the stew on Father's Day, proceed as follows:

3:45   Start the stew.

Any time between 4 and 6 prepare the carrots and open the cans. Also prepare French bread with garlic butter.

6:00   Add carrots to stew.

6:01   Prepare apple crunch.

6:30   Cook green beans.

6:35   Preheat oven to 375 degrees.

6:40   Put bread into oven. Remove when golden. Put potatoes in at the same time.

6:45   Add tomatoes, kidney beans, and green beans to stew.

6:50   Thicken gravy.

6:55   Put apple crunch into oven. Set timer for 7:30 so that if the family hasn't finished dinner you won't forget to turn off the oven and keep the dessert warm until needed. Serve the main course.

When it is finished, serve the apple crunch.

DUTCH OVEN

PARTY BEEF
STEW

2 pounds rump of beef, cut in 1-inch cubes
Salt and pepper
2 tablespoons butter (or more, if needed)
4 medium onions, sliced
Paprika for sprinkling
3 cups beef stock, made with bouillon cubes or powdered beef stock
1 large bunch carrots
2 cups water
1 teaspoon chili powder
1 teaspoon paprika
1 1-pound, 13-ounce can tomatoes
2 packages frozen Frenched green beans, cooked according to package directions
1 1-pound can kidney beans
3 tablespoons cornstarch
½ pint chilled sour cream

Pat beef dry with paper towels. This makes it brown more easily. Sprinkle with salt and pepper. Brown well in butter on all sides, in a large pot or Dutch oven. Add onions and sprinkle well with paprika. Allow onions to brown lightly. Add beef stock and simmer gently, covered, for 2 hours. Scrape the carrots and slice them lengthwise. Add to the beef at the end of two hours with water, chili powder, and the teaspoon of paprika. Cook gently until carrots are tender (35–45 minutes). Add tomatoes, kidney beans with their liquid, and green beans. Heat well. Blend cornstarch with a few tablespoonsful of the gravy. Stir into the stew. Serve piping hot in a heated dish with a bowl of the chilled sour cream sprinkled with paprika to spoon over each serving. *Serves 6.*

POTATOES AU GRATIN

Make mashed potatoes for six according to package directions on box of mashed potato mix. Put into a casserole and cover the top with grated Cheddar cheese (about 1 cup). Bake in 375 degree oven until cheese is golden brown (about 20 minutes).

GARLIC FRENCH BREAD

1 loaf brown-and-serve French bread
¼ cup (½ stick) butter, softened
1 clove garlic, mashed (or ¼ teaspoon garlic powder)

Take the butter from the refrigerator at least a half hour before you mean to use it so that it will soften at room temperature. Put it into a small bowl, add garlic or garlic powder and mix very thoroughly. Slice a loaf of brown-and-serve French bread (unbaked) from the top crust almost down to the bottom crust, but not quite. With a flat knife, put garlic butter between each of the slices. If there's any left over, spread it on top of the bread. Bake in 375 degree oven until golden (15–20 minutes). Wrap in a napkin to serve.

APPLE CRUNCH

3 pounds cooking apples (McIntosh are fine)
1 cup flour
½ cup sugar
½ cup (1 stick) butter
Nutmeg

Peel, core, and slice apples and place in a buttered baking dish. Mix flour and sugar well. Mix them to a paste with the butter. Spread over the top of the apples. Sprinkle with nutmeg. Bake in 375 degree oven 35 minutes. Serve with whipped cream (see page 201) if desired. *Serves 6.*

After Graduation Party

Graduation day is a big milestone in your lives and some celebration is certainly indicated. Why not invite a good-sized group of your friends for late supper at your house, served in buffet style? Give everybody a chance to go home and change to informal clothes, if they like. Meantime, you can start your very simple preparation for the party. Depending upon what time the graduation festivities will end, you can set the hour for your party. Certainly, with all the excitement and the great feeling which comes from the realization that there'll be no more exams or work for at least a little while, nobody wants to go to bed early. So get together a good collection of favorite records and have a dance before and after your supper.

MENU	**Scrambled Eggs**
For Twelve	**Little Sausages**
	Heated Croissants and Brioches
	Apricot Jam
	Strawberry Whip **Rolled Vanilla Cookies**
	Coffee **Milk**

Market List	2½ dozen eggs 3 pounds fresh pork sausage links 2 packages croissants 2 packages brioches 1 pint strawberries 1 package rolled vanilla cookies
Check These Staples	Butter (about 3 sticks, including that for buttering the brioches and croissants) Salt Pepper Superfine sugar (2 cups)
Utensils Needed	2 large skillets for eggs Forks for stirring eggs 1 or 2 large shallow baking pans for sausages Tongs for turning sausages Large bowl for strawberry whip Electric mixer or rotary beater

TIMING *If supper is to be served at 11 o'clock*

In the morning or early afternoon make the strawberry whip. Refrigerate.

10:15 Arrange sausages in their pans.

10:20 Preheat oven to 400 degrees.

10:30 Place sausages in oven. Turn with tongs occasionally to brown all sides.

10:40 Start scrambling eggs.

10:45 Place croissants and brioches in oven. Check occasionally to see that they don't overbrown.

10:55 The eggs should take about fifteen minutes if your heat is properly low. When exactly to your liking, stir in the extra egg yolks and put into whatever serving device you intend to use.

STRAWBERRY
WHIP
1 pint strawberries

2 cups superfine sugar

2 egg whites at room temperature (save yolks for tonight)

Put all ingredients into a bowl and beat with electric mixer or rotary beater until stiff enough to hold their shape (15 minutes with mixer—30 minutes with rotary beater). The ingredients will at least triple in bulk. Refrigerate until ready to serve. *Serves 12.*

LITTLE
SAUSAGES
3 pounds fresh pork sausage links

Arrange links in shallow baking pan or pans. Do not pile up. Bake in 400 degree oven until nicely browned, turning occasionally with tongs (20–30 minutes). *Serves 12.*

SCRAMBLED
EGGS

I would suggest that you press one of your guests into helping you with the making of these, because if you try to cook all these eggs in one pan and do it, as you should, over a low heat, it will take forever. The object of adding the extra egg yolks just before serving is that if the eggs have to stand even a little while before they're eaten this will keep them moist and soft as they should be.

24 eggs

½ cup (1 stick) butter

Salt and pepper to taste
2 raw egg yolks

Melt half of the butter in each of two large skillets. Break 12 of the eggs into each pan and cook over low heat, stirring constantly with a fork, until eggs are just set and still soft. eason to taste. Stir a raw egg yolk into each batch of scram- ed eggs and serve them on a hot platter, kept warm on a t tray or in a chafing dish or in dishes over hot water. rves 12.

HEATED
CROISSANTS
AND
BRIOCHES

Buy these in packages and heat according to directions on package in their own foil pans. Serve wrapped in napkins, in baskets if you have them.

Fourth of July—

AT THE OUTDOOR GRILL

After the parade, perhaps around one o'clock, on the Fourth of July is a great time to have an outdoor cooking party. Or, if you'd prefer, you could set it for late afternoon or early evening, which might be cooler. In any case it's an informal, fun kind of party for all concerned and equally appealing to boys or girls. Though men are inclined to regard outdoor grill cooking as their province, I have known many females who were equally good at it, and there's one thing I'm sure of—anyone can do this kind of cooking if he will just obey the simple rules regarding the fire, the distance from it upon which foods are cooked, and the length of time required.

Although nothing could be better than frankfurters or hamburgers grilled over glowing coals, you will notice that I not only give you recipes for doing those two simple bits of cooking, but also for making stuffed frankfurters and stuffed hamburgers, just in case you'd like to provide a surprise note with either, or both, of them. They're fun, but not a bit necessary if you're feeling lazy.

There's a great factor about this kind of party of which you should take every advantage. It's easy to share the work. For instance, you might put one guest in charge of tending the fire, thus releasing yourself to do other tasks. Get several people to husk the corn. Get several to help carry the food out. This will make everything go smoothly as long as you pay attention to the time schedule and see that those responsible do their parts when they're supposed to.

MENU
For Eight

Frankfurters (or stuffed frankfurters)
Hamburgers (or stuffed hamburgers)
Frankfurter rolls   Hamburger rolls
Mustard   Pickle Relish
Corn on the Cob
Cole Slaw
Ice Cream Cones   Cookies
Milk   Coffee

Market List

1 large firm head of cabbage
16 ears corn
8 frankfurters
8 frankfurter rolls
4 ounces chive or vegetable cottage cheese (if stuffed frankfurters are served)
2½ pounds ground bottom round (or 2 pounds if stuffed hamburgers are served)
8 hamburger buns
3 or 4 pints different flavors of ice cream
16 ice cream cones
Box of cookies (or check ingredients for making chocolate morsel ones on page 182)

Check These Staples

Onions (½ cup chopped for coleslaw and ¼ cup if stuffed hamburgers are served)

Salt

Pepper

Mayonnaise (½ to ¾ cup)

Butter

Bacon (8 slices if stuffed frankfurters are served)

All-purpose barbecue sauce with hickory smoke flavor (if stuffed frankfurters are served)

Eggs (2)

All-purpose barbecue sauce (1 cup if stuffed hamburgers are served)

Pickle relish (¼ cup)

Cheddar cheese (¼ cup grated if stuffed hamburgers are served)

Utensils Needed

Frankfurter holder or 2-sided wire broiler for franks

2-sided wire broiler for hamburgers

Knife for splitting buns

Knife for buttering buns

Tongs for turning corn (if done on grill)

Large pot for corn (if done in the house)

Measuring cup

Measuring spoons

Cheese grater (for stuffed hamburgers)

Fork for beating eggs

Heavy duty foil

Basting brush

Asbestos gloves

Foil pan (for stuffed frankfurters)

Ice cream scoop

Lots of paper napkins (red, white, and blue, of course!)

TIMING
10:45

If meal is to be grilled at 1 P.M.
(or early in the morning if you prefer)
Make cole slaw.

11:05	Prepare hamburgers (and frankfurters, if they're to be stuffed). Refrigerate.
11:30	Start fire if of wood.
12:00	Start fire if of briquets.
12:10	Husk corn and prepare for cooking.
12:35	Put corn on fire, if it's to be roasted; *or* start water boiling in covered pot if it's to be done on the range.
12:50	Put corn into water and bring back to boil *uncovered*.
1:00	Take all food but ice cream to the grill and picnic area.
1:05	Cook hamburgers and frankfurters.

THE
FIRE

The most important thing in outdoor cooking is the fire. Whatever fuel you use, the fire must be started sufficiently ahead of the moment at which you wish to cook so that you get a good bed of glowing coals to cook over. If your fuel is wood, the fire should be started an hour before you're going to use it. If you use charcoal or briquets, you should start the fire 30 minutes before if you want those glowing coals.

A wood fire should be made with hard wood such as oak, hickory, or fruit wood. You must build it at the start with all the wood you intend to use. It should not be disturbed while cooking is going on. Adding more wood and poking at the fire break up the retention of heat in the gas pockets formed by the burning wood.

Most people nowadays use briquets for outdoor cooking. This is a far easier fire to manage than a wood one. You can add more briquets without disturbing your fire. The best thing about them is that they are uniform in size, clean, and they burn well and long. Lump charcoal is likely to be in pieces of various sizes which makes an uneven firebed. So use briquets if you can.

As for kindling, use newspaper that is well crumpled, surrounded by small sticks of soft wood built into a teepee shape for air circulation. Light this and when it is burning merrily, add five or six briquets or a couple of logs and when they start burning, add the remaining fuel you're using. A fire of briquets is ready when they show a white ash. You can also, if it is available to you, use a commercial fire starter. Odorless paint thinner is excellent for the purpose and not as expensive as some of those made specifically for barbecuing.

COLE SLAW

1 large firm head of cabbage
½ cup finely chopped onion (made from instant dehydrated if you like)
Salt and pepper to taste
½ to ¾ cup mayonnaise (to taste) or use a prepared coleslaw mix

Cut the cabbage in half and remove the hard core. Shred or chop the rest of the cabbage. Mix with onion, salt and pepper, and enough mayonnaise to suit your taste. Chill thoroughly in a bowl in the refrigerator. *Serves 8.*

CORN ON
THE COB

16 ears corn
Butter
Salt and pepper

Husk corn, season with salt and pepper and spread with butter. Double wrap each ear in heavy duty aluminum foil. Place on coals and roast for about 25 minutes, turning two or three times. If you haven't a large enough grill to accommodate the wrapped ears and at the same time allow you to grill your meat, husk the corn and plunge it into boiling, salted water in a large kettle in the kitchen. When water returns to the boil, cook 3 minutes. Drain corn, cover kettle, and bring it to the picnic table as is, serving plenty of butter for the guests to add themselves. *Serves 8.*

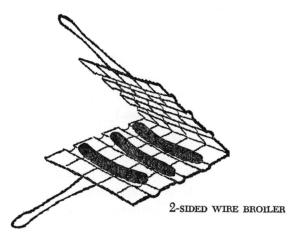

2-SIDED WIRE BROILER

FRANKFURTERS

8 frankfurters
8 frankfurter rolls
Butter

Put frankfurters into a special frankfurter holder or a 2-sided wire broiler and cook 4 inches from fire bed, turning frequently, until browned to your liking and heated through. Split rolls and toast them on the grill. Butter them and serve a frankfurter in each. *Serves 8 (if you're also having hamburgers).*

STUFFED FRANKFURTERS

8 frankfurters
1 cup chive or vegetable cottage cheese
8 bacon slices
1 cup all-purpose barbecue sauce with hickory smoke flavor
8 frankfurter rolls
Butter

Slit frankfurters lengthwise to ½ inch from each end. Stuff each with about 2 tablespoons cottage cheese. Wind a bacon slice around each frankfurter, securing it with a toothpick at each end. Place in a foil pan on the grill about 4 inches from the heat and cook, turning frequently, until bacon is cooked to your taste on all sides. Brush with barbecue sauce and cook about 5 minutes longer, or until frankfurters are well glazed. Meantime, split rolls and toast them on the grill. Butter them and serve a frankfurter in each. *Serves 8 (if you're also serving hamburgers).*

To cook indoors: Prepare as above. Bake on a rack set in a pan in a 400 degree oven 20 minutes. Pour barbecue sauce over frankfurters and bake 10 minutes longer or until frankfurters are glazed.

HAMBURGERS
2½ pounds ground bottom round
2 eggs
Salt and pepper to taste
8 hamburger buns
Butter

Mix meat, eggs, and seasonings with hands, thoroughly but lightly. Form into 8 thick cakes if you like hamburgers rare or into 8 thin cakes if you like them well done. Lay the cakes in a 2-sided wire broiler and sear them quickly 3 inches from the fire bed on the first side. Quickly sear the other side. Test for rareness by making a cut well down into the thickest part and pulling it gently apart. Hamburgers do not take as long to cook as you might expect. This one requires about 8 minutes in all to be nicely rare. Split hamburger buns and toast on the grill. Butter and serve a hamburger on each.
To cook indoors: Prepare as above. Cook in broiler at 400 degrees 4 inches from heat about 3 minutes on each side, or until browned.

HAMBURGERS STUFFED
2 pounds ground bottom round
¼ cup all-purpose barbecue sauce
2 eggs, slightly beaten
½ teaspoon salt
¾ cup all-purpose barbecue sauce
¼ cup grated or finely chopped Cheddar cheese
¼ cup pickle relish
¼ cup chopped onion
8 hamburger buns

Combine beef, the ¼ cup barbecue sauce, eggs, and salt and mix lightly. Divide into 16 parts and gently shape each into a thin round patty. Place about 1 teaspoon each of barbecue sauce, cheese, relish, and onion on 8 of the patties. Top with remaining patties and gently press the edges together to seal in the filling. Broil 4 inches from heat for about 4 minutes. Turn, baste with remaining barbecue sauce and continue cooking 4 minutes longer or until meat is of desired doneness. Meantime, split and toast the buns. Serve a stuffed hamburger in each. *Serves 8.*

To cook indoors: Broil 4 inches from 400 degree heat or fry in butter about 3 minutes on one side. Turn, baste with remaining barbecue sauce, and continue cooking 3 minutes longer, or until of desired doneness.

ICE CREAM
CONES

All you need to serve these is an ice cream scoop, a choice of two or three flavors of ice cream, and the best cones you can buy—the crisp variety, not those awful ones that taste like pressed tissue paper! Better allow two cones per person and a pint of each kind of ice cream, which you will bring out from the house when the rest of the meal has been consumed.

COOKIES

Make these, if you like, perhaps the chocolate chip ones on page 182. Or serve packaged or bakery ones. They are on the menu just to serve as extra nibbling foods.

A Beach Picnic

A beach picnic, or one to be taken to the woods, for that matter, offers one of the best chances for setting up a cooperative party. In other words, each of the picnickers contributes one part of the menu. This necessitates having one person who plans and coordinates the whole matter. Let's say that's you. First you decide how many varieties of sandwich you want and whether you want other foods as well for your main course. This can be done in consultation with others of the party, but remember that in taking on the responsibility for seeing that all gets done you also must be ready to retain some suggestions and discard others or the whole thing can turn into a shambles. By and large, if it's a picnic for boys and girls, assign the boys items they can go out and buy—soft drinks (if you have any way to keep them cold), fruit, ready-made cookies or cake, and the like. However, if you're lucky enough to have an outstanding cook or sandwich maker among the boys, by all means let him do his thing which may be better than anyone else would be able to dream up.

If you're setting up a picnic for four, two kinds of sandwiches (four of each), plus some other interesting accom-

paniments, are plenty. If the party is for twelve, arrange to
have six each of four different kinds. Since they will be cut
in half each guest can try all of them if he wants to, or if
there's one kind he doesn't like and another he goes for in
a big way, he can concentrate on the latter and enjoy himself thoroughly.

A picnic which includes cold broiled chicken requires only
one or two very simple types of sandwich to accompany the
main attraction—bread-and-butter, cucumber, or something
like them. On the other hand, if the picnic is based on Heros
(or whatever your part of the country calls them—poor boys,
grinders, etc.) just a few raw vegetables and perhaps pickles
and olives will round out the meal perfectly.

If your family or the family of anybody who's participating
owns one of those portable iceboxes (into which you put tins
of "canned ice"), you're truly in luck. It will keep cold food
refreshing and delicious until you're ready to eat. You can
also take your own soft drinks and have them cold in case
you're planning to picnic far from any place where you could
buy them already iced. However, if you have no access to
such a fine accessory, you can make out perfectly well, as
people have for years, with boxes and thermoses.

In addition to the basic containers mentioned above you
will need paper napkins—plenty of them—salt, pepper, paper
plates (coated with plastic if possible), paper cups for either
hot or cold drinks, knives for cutting up certain foods, and a
bottle opener. Also close at hand when the container is being
packed—whatever variety it may be—you should have the
menu, plus a list of the necessary accessories so that you may
check them off as you put them in and not suddenly find
yourselves miles from home without some of the food or a
bottle opener or some other vital part of the picnic.

Here is a collection of sandwiches good for taking on a

beach picnic, from which you may choose any two or more you like for your party. In each case, the quantities suggested are for four; but you have only to multiply them for the numbers involved if you have more, since it isn't like multiplying the ingredients in, for instance, a recipe for baked goods, which isn't likely to work out right at all.

SANDWICH POSSIBILITIES

One important point to remember is to vary the breads upon which you construct your sandwiches. There's an almost infinite variety to choose from, so let your imagination roam and decide just what would taste the very best with the fillings you've chosen. There's nothing wrong with good white bread, and for certain fillings it seems the only possibility, but appetite depends a lot on variety so don't forget the other kinds.

1. **Baked Bean Sandwiches:** 1 cup canned baked beans, drained, 2 tablespoons pickle relish, 1 tablespoon mayonnaise, 8 slices Boston brown bread, butter, 4 slices bologna. Combine beans with pickle and mayonnaise, mixing well. Spread bread slices with butter. Place bean mixture on half of the bread slices. Top each with a slice of bologna. Top with remaining bread slices. Cut sandwiches in half. Wrap carefully in sandwich bags and refrigerate until just ready to go on the picnic. *Makes 4 sandwiches.*

2. **Heros:** 4 loaves brown-and-serve French bread, butter, 12 thin slices salami, 8 thin slices Swiss cheese, 4 large lettuce leaves. Bake the bread just in time to let it cool before making the sandwiches. Slit each loaf in half lengthwise. Butter.

Lay four slices of salami and two slices of cheese on each bottom slice, folding the cheese, if necessary. Tear the lettuce so that it will fit in neatly and lay it on the cheese. Lay tops of breads on this. Cut in half diagonally. Wrap in foil or plastic wrap and pack in lunch box. Be sure to take along in little jars mustard, pickles, and whatever else you like on your Heros. *Makes 4 Heros.*

3. Tunafish Salad Sandwiches: 1 7-ounce can tunafish, drained and flaked, 2 tablespoons minced green pepper, 1 tablespoon minced onion, 2 tablespoons minced celery, ⅓ cup mayonnaise, 1 tablespoon chili sauce (optional), 4 lettuce leaves, 8 slices protein or whole wheat bread. Mix tunafish with vegetables, mayonnaise, and chili sauce (if used). Spread on four of the bread slices. Cover with remaining bread slices. Cut sandwiches in half. Wrap well in sandwich bags and store in refrigerator until just before going on the picnic. *Makes 4 sandwiches.*

4. Cucumber Sandwiches: 1 medium cucumber, 2 tablespoons mayonnaise, freshly ground black pepper, 8 thin slices white bread. Peel the cucumber and slice paper thin into a bowl of salted ice water. Let stand 10–15 minutes. Drain well and pat dry on paper toweling. Spread mayonnaise on the bread. Lay cucumber slices on half of the bread slices. Sprinkle with freshly ground black pepper to taste. Top with remaining bread slices. Cut sandwiches in half. Wrap well in sandwich bags and refrigerate until just before going on the picnic. *Makes 4 sandwiches.*

5. Cold Meat Sandwiches: If you are lucky enough to have cold roast beef, ham, tongue, lamb, chicken, or turkey in the house, they make wonderful sandwiches. Butter the bread upon which you make them and either take along separately or spread on them condiments which match them well: mustard, chili sauce or ketchup, horseradish (especially for beef), pickle relish, jelly (mint on the lamb, perhaps), or mayonnaise (especially on chicken).

6. Cheese Sandwiches: There's scarcely a cheese in the world which can't go into the making of a good sandwich—if it happens to be a cheese you like. Cheddar and Swiss are probably the most popular, and may I point out that if you buy them in a hunk and slice off what you want just as you make the sandwiches, they will be far better than if you buy the cheese sliced. Don't forget that Swiss cheese and ham make a "combination" sandwich, one of the best liked of all time and especially good on rye bread. Butter any bread to be used for cheese sandwiches, as that keeps them moist. Many of the same condiments which go well with meat sandwiches are good with cheese.

7. Meat Loaf Sandwiches: Cold meat loaf makes fine sandwiches. Slice it fairly thin, place on a slice of buttered bread, spread with ketchup or chili sauce and top with another slice of buttered bread. Cut sandwiches in half. Wrap well in sandwich bags and refrigerate until just ready to leave for the picnic.

8. Apple and Ham Sandwiches: 8 slices white bread, butter, 8 thin slices boiled ham, 16 thin slices unpeeled red apple, fresh lemon juice. Spread bread with butter. On 4 of the slices place 2 slices boiled ham each. Top each with 4 slices apple. Sprinkle with lemon juice to preserve the color. Cover with remaining bread slices. Cut sandwiches in half. Wrap well in sandwich bags and refrigerate until going on the picnic. *Makes 4 sandwiches.*

9. Bologna and Egg Sandwiches: 2 hard-cooked eggs, salt and pepper, 2 tablespoons ketchup, 8 slices protein or whole wheat bread, butter, 16 thin slices bologna. Shell and chop eggs and season with salt and pepper. Mix with ketchup. Spread bread generously with butter. Place 4 thin slices of bologna on each of 4 bread slices. Top with egg mixture. Cover with remaining bread slices. Cut sandwiches in half. Wrap well in sandwich bags and refrigerate until time to go on the picnic. *Makes 4 sandwiches.*

10. Peanut Butter Sandwiches: You may react with, "Who doesn't know about them?" but I just want to remind you of all the things you can add to make them less dry and more interesting. Add crumbled bacon and a bit of mayonnaise; add applesauce and chopped celery and mix well before spreading; add jelly or jam; top with pot cheese mixed with chopped chives; mix with orange marmalade and add a slice of Cheddar cheese to each; combine with chopped pimiento and chopped green peppers, top each with a slice of Swiss cheese; mix with crushed pineapple; top with peeled orange slices before adding second slice of bread.

11. Cream Cheese Sandwiches: Cream cheese is marvelous by itself on date-nut bread. First smooth and soften it with a little milk or light cream so that it spreads easily. It is also a great base for imaginative additions and changes, such as: mix with chopped nuts or pimiento; mix with stewed apricots which have been mashed in the blender; combine with an equal amount of chopped beets; combine with chopped celery, including leaves; combine with chopped celery and dates; combine with chopped figs; add enough liquid honey to make spreading consistency, sprinkle with chopped nuts; spread cream cheese on one slice and jelly on the other, put together; mix with chopped stuffed olives, moisten with French dressing to make of spreading consistency; combine with an equal quantity of chopped water cress, season with salt, pepper, and a dash of Worcestershire.

12. Special Shrimp Sandwiches: 3 tablespoons butter, 1 tablespoon lemon juice, 1 tablespoon finely chopped onion, 1 teaspoon finely chopped parsley, dash of Worcestershire sauce, dash Tabasco, dash pepper, 1 cup finely chopped cooked or canned shrimp, 8 slices rye bread, 4 lettuce leaves. Combine butter, lemon juice, onion, parsley, Worcestershire, Tabasco, and pepper. Stir in shrimp. Spread on 4 slices of the bread and top each with a lettuce leaf, then the remaining bread slices. Cut each sandwich in half. Wrap carefully in sandwich bags and refrigerate until ready to go on the picnic. *Makes 4 sandwiches.*

AND IN ADDITION

1. Cold Chicken: Cook "oven-broiled chicken" (page 31) the day before the picnic. Cool, wrap each piece in foil or plastic wrap, and refrigerate until ready to go on the picnic. Allow either a half or a quarter chicken per person. You know the appetites of your friends best, but remember people are likely to be might hungry after swimming.

2. Deviled Eggs: Cook enough hard-cooked eggs (see page 199) to provide one for each picnicker. Cool and chill them. Shell and cut in half, lengthwise. Remove yolks to a small bowl, being careful to keep the whites intact. Mash yolks, season with salt and pepper, and add mayonnaise enough to hold them together. Be careful not to add too much or they will be too "gooey" for finger food. You may add a dash of curry, mustard, Worcestershire, chopped parsley, a bit of chopped ham, chopped pickle, or a little anchovy paste to the basic deviled eggs for variety and interest.

3. **Hard-Cooked Eggs:** Perhaps you'd prefer to take these, rather than go through the deviling process. If so, see page 199. Cool them and chill them well before packing in the picnic box. And take along seasoned salt to dip them in at the picnic.

4. Raw Vegetables: Carrots, celery, sweet red or green pepper, cut into sticks, radishes, scallions, cherry tomatoes, or any other vegetable you like to eat raw can add a nice crisp crunch and a lot of color to your picnic fare. Seasoned salt is good to dunk them in too, or take a little container of mixed salt and pepper.

5. Condiments: Take what goes best with the basic food: mustard, ketchup, chili sauce, pickle relish, pickles (gherkins or big dills), olives, salt and pepper are all possibilities.

IN THE THERMOS

If it's hot liquid you're taking in the thermos, fill the bottles or jugs with hot water for a while before pouring in the eventual contents. If it's cold, be sure to include plenty of ice, except in the case of milk shakes, which must be well chilled before being poured into the thermos.

Hot Drinks in the Thermos: Soup is perhaps the ideal hot drink. Choose a type which is not too full of solid bits, perhaps a cream of tomato or green pea. But if you prefer vegetable or green pea with bits of ham in it, be sure to shake the thermos before pouring it into the cups so that the solids are not all sunk to the bottom. You can also, of course, take hot coffee, or hot cocoa.

Cold Drinks in the Thermos: Milk or flavored milk shakes lead the list if you're not to be where you can buy them handily. In addition, you might take lemonade, orangeade, iced vegetable or tomato juice, iced tea or coffee, or fruit punch (made from a mix). Where appropriate, take along lemon wedges to squeeze into certain drinks, sprigs of mint to pop into others, and any other additions you like for whatever drink you've chosen.

DESSERTS

Cookies, plain cakes, or fruit are the best choices. Try to plan in any of these categories things which are not too gooey or juicy, as all the paper napkins in the world won't help if your desserts drip all over you. It's easy to make or buy un-gooey cookies. As for cakes, the best choices are pound cake, sponge, or angel cake (without icing). In fruit, apples, pears, bananas are fine, plums and such fruits are too drippy.

Market List

In this particular instance, you're on your own entirely. Decide what foods you're going to take, make out a menu, and from that make a check list of staples and a market list. Do your shopping at least a day ahead.

TIMING

Once again, it's impossible for me to make a timing schedule for you, as I don't know what you've chosen for your picnic. However, it should not be hard for you to do, as you will just allow plenty of hours or minutes to prepare everything well ahead and have only the packing to do just before you set forth. Make your sandwiches early in the morning, or make them the night before so they may chill thoroughly in the refrigerator before they're packed. *Or* make the sandwiches and freeze them the day before. This is a particularly good thing to do if you haven't an "ice box," because they will just about thaw out by lunch time at the beach, if you've packed them frozen, and will thus be cool and delicious. However, do not freeze any sandwich which has mayonnaise in it, as that condiment doesn't freeze well.

Things like hard-cooked eggs and broiled chicken should be prepared the day before. If the eggs are to be deviled that should, ideally, be done the morning of the picnic as they will taste fresher and better. Raw vegetables can be cleaned, cut into sticks if desired, and refrigerated in ice water to crisp, also on the day before the picnic.

FUTURES

Don't forget (I'm sure you won't) that sandwiches make excellent snack food if you're ravenously hungry. You can also use these suggestions for making sandwiches to take for lunch at school. If you do, try the system of having a Big Sandwich Making once a week, then freezing them, well wrapped. Take them from the freezer each day, just as you're starting out, and they will just defrost nicely by lunch time.

After the Football Game

Because my friend Margot says, "Don't suggest too much for this one, because we all eat so much at the game," I have kept the menu to a bare, but delicious, minimum. It consists of things you couldn't get in any stadium, so, in any case, it will be a change from what you've been eating all afternoon! If you're not hungry when you first get home, play some games or do a little dancing until appetites return, then set to on this very easy supper.

MENU
For Eight

Sloppy Joes

Carrot Sticks   Cherry Tomatoes

Green Pepper Sticks

Seasoned Salt

Hot Cocoa

Cup Cakes (for those who must have a sweet)

Market List
2 pounds chopped chuck
2 envelopes Sloppy Joe mix
1 6-ounce can tomato paste
8 hamburger buns
Bunch of carrots
Basket of cherry tomatoes
2 green peppers
8 cup cakes or a layer cake or cookies

Check These Staples
Seasoned salt
Milk (at least 2 quarts)
Instant cocoa

Utensils Needed
Saucepan for Sloppy Joes
Measuring cup
Vegetable peeler
Paring knife
Double boiler for heating milk

TIMING *If supper is to be served at 7*

Before you go to the game, prepare the Sloppy Joe mix and the raw vegetables. Allow half to three quarters of an hour for completing both.

6:30 Reheat Sloppy Joe mixture.

6:35 Split hamburger buns.

6:45 Put milk on to heat in double boiler.

6:50 Dry vegetables on paper towels and arrange on serving plate.

7:00 Serve the dinner—put on everything, including the cake or cookies, as this is a buffet-style party.

SLOPPY JOES

When I discovered that there's an excellent Sloppy Joe mixture in an envelope, I thought I'd try it and perhaps add a few twists to improve it. It's so exactly right, I couldn't! So I offer you one of the easiest (and best) Sloppy Joes of all time and am sure you'll love it—and so will your guests.

> 2 pounds chopped chuck
> 2 envelopes Sloppy Joe mix
> 1 6-ounce can tomato paste
> 8 hamburger buns, split

Prepare the Sloppy Joes exactly as directed on the package. You can do this before you go to the game and reheat the mixture when you're ready to serve. It reheats beautifully. Serve in a big bowl with arrangements to keep it hot. Have a toaster on the buffet table so that each guest can toast his own bun and spoon the meat over it. *Serves 8.*

RAW VEGETABLES

> 4 carrots
> 16 cherry tomatoes
> 2 green peppers

Before the game, scrape the carrots and cut them into sticks. Wash the tomatoes. Cut the peppers in half and remove seeds and membrane, then cut them into sticks. Put all into a bowl of cold water and refrigerate. When ready to serve, dry on paper toweling and place attractively on a plate or platter with a small dish of seasoned salt in the center for dunking.

HOT
COCOA

2 quarts milk, heated
Instant cocoa

I suggest that you produce a large pot of hot milk on the
buffet table, plus a container of instant cocoa and let each
guest concoct his own to the strength he likes. 2 quarts of
milk will give you eight cupfuls.

CUP
CAKES

You may feel that any sort of "dessert" is one too many for
this meal, in which case, forget the whole thing. But if you
have sweet-toothed friends, you'd better buy either cup cakes
or a layer cake or cookies to satisfy their craving. This will
undoubtedly be too busy a day for you to make anything of
the sort yourself, what with fixing the vegetables and the
Sloppy Joe mix and getting yourself ready to go to the game.
Have fun!

Halloween Party

Everybody, of whatever age, loves a Halloween party. The possibilities for decoration are practically limitless and things you make yourself are without doubt the best of all. Making jack-o'-lanterns is great fun, and they will provide the base for some fine pumpkin pies! Perhaps you will want to use one for the centerpiece of your table, in which case how about a black paper tablecloth, orange candles, and orange paper napkins—perhaps with witches or ghosts on them? Halloween masks make weird and effective coverings for wall lights. And of course you'll ask everyone to come in costume, perhaps offering a prize for the most original. Some of the old traditional Halloween games are just as much fun for young adults as for children: bobbing for apples—such a delightfully messy performance—apple-on-a-string, or raisin-on-a-string are examples. Great fun, especially if it's a party for both boys and girls.

MENU Ghostly Brew
For Ten Snack Crackers
Witches' Burgers
Jack-o'-Lantern Salad
Vanilla Ice Cream with Apricot Jam Sauce
Halloween Cookies
Coffee   Milk

Market List
2 large heads Boston lettuce
5 large oranges
Ripe olives (10)
1 quart ginger ale
1 1-pint, 2-fluid ounce can pineapple juice
1 bottle cranberry juice
1 pint lemon ice
1 pound ground beef
2 1-pound cans pork and beans
1 bottle all-purpose barbecue sauce
10 hamburger buns
2 quarts vanilla ice cream
1 12-ounce jar apricot jam
Licorice candy for accent in cookies

Check These Staples
Flour
Baking powder
Salt
Butter (¾ cup—1½ sticks)
Sugar
Egg (1)
Vanilla
Milk
Olive oil
Vinegar
Pepper
Onions (2)

Utensils   Can opener
Needed   Bowl for dry ingredients
Bowl for butter mixture
Mixing spoons
Foil or plastic wrap
Pastry board (with cloth, if possible)
Rolling pin (with "sleeve," if possible)
Halloween cookie cutters
Baking sheet or sheets
Clean tea towel
Paring knife
Bowl for salad dressing
Ice cream scoop
Skillet for burgers
Fork
Toaster
Double boiler
Punch bowl

TIMING   *If meal is to be served at 7*

In the morning (or the afternoon before) make the cookies.

6:00   Wash lettuce, shake to remove excess moisture, and wrap in a clean tea towel. Refrigerate.

Prepare orange and olive slices and refrigerate them.

6:30   Make Ghostly Brew and serve to guests with snack crackers as soon as they arrive.

6:35   Put jam and water into double boiler and place over low heat.

6:40   Prepare salad.

6:50   Prepare Witches' Burgers and get a guest to toast the buns.

Serve.

When the main course is finished, serve the ice cream and cookies.

HALLOWEEN
COOKIES

1 recipe for sugar cookies (see page 201)

You'll need Halloween cookie cutters for these—witch, pumpkin, or whatever you have or can find in the dime store. They really should be iced (for icing see page 203), as the colors are important. You can have great fun applying the icing to make the appropriate designs in orange and white. Use licorice candy for black accents.

JACK-O'-
LANTERN
SALAD
2 large heads Boston lettuce
5 large oranges
10 ripe olives (about)
½ cup olive oil
¼ cup vinegar
Salt and pepper to taste

Wash lettuce, shake to remove excess moisture, wrap in a clean tea towel, and refrigerate to crisp. When ready to prepare, arrange lettuce leaves on each of ten salad plates (Halloween paper ones would be great). Peel oranges and slice each into four slices. Place two slices on each plate. Cut the olives into pieces which will enable you to make eyes, nose and mouth on the orange slices to turn them into jack-o'-lanterns. Mix oil, vinegar, salt and pepper and pour over the salads. *Serves 10.*

GHOSTLY BREW

1 quart ginger ale
1 1-pint, 2-fluid ounce can pineapple juice
1 bottle cranberry juice
1 pint lemon ice

Chill ginger ale and fruit juices thoroughly. Pour over ice in a punch bowl and float scoops of lemon ice on top. *Makes about 16 punch cups.*

WITCHES' BURGERS

2 medium onions, chopped
¼ cup (½ stick) butter
1 pound ground beef
3 teaspoons salt
2 1-pound cans pork and beans or baked beans (or use red kidney beans and omit water)
1 cup all-purpose barbecue sauce
½ cup water
10 hamburger buns, split and toasted

Sauté onion in butter in skillet until tender but not browned. Add beef and cook until browned, breaking up meat with a fork as it cooks. Add salt, beans, barbecue sauce, and water. Simmer 5 minutes. Serve on toasted buns. *Makes 7 cups meat mixture or 10 servings.*

VANILLA ICE CREAM WITH APRICOT JAM SAUCE

1 12-ounce jar apricot jam
½ cup water
2 quarts vanilla ice cream

In a double boiler heat the jam, well mixed with the water. When ready to serve, pour it over vanilla ice cream in individual dishes. *Serves 10.*

Dinner for the Saturday after Thanksgiving

This dinner will be based on leftover turkey and, hopefully, the remains of the big bowl of fruit that decorated the table on "turkey day." There is really very little extra work to be done, so why not make some cornbread to set off the meal in style? You can do it from a mix if you like (they're very good) or from scratch from the recipe given below.

MENU	Turkey and Macaroni Casserole
For Four	Broccoli
	Corn Bread
	Fresh Fruit Bowl
	Coffee Milk

Market List	1 8-ounce can sliced mushrooms
	1 bunch broccoli (about 1½ pounds)
	½ pint sour cream (if you have persimmons)

Check These Staples
Cooked turkey (2 cups, cut up coarsely)
Macaroni (8 oz.)
Chicken bouillon cube or powdered chicken stock
Light cream (½ cup)
Butter (about 1½ sticks)
Flour
Salt
Pepper
Grated cheese (½ cup)
Yellow cornmeal (1 cup)
Baking powder
Sugar
Milk (1 cup)
Egg (1)

Utensils Needed
Measuring cups
Measuring spoons
Saucepan for casserole sauce
Mixing spoon
Saucepan for cooking macaroni
Casserole
Cheese grater
Paring knife
Pot to fit broccoli
Collander
Small saucepan for melting butter
Sifter
Bowl for mixing cornbread
Small bowl for milk mixture
Mixing spoon
Square pan for cornbread
Knife for cutting cornbread

TIMING *If dinner is to be served at 7*
6:00 Put turkey casserole together.
6:20 Preheat oven to 375 degrees.
6:21 Prepare cornbread.
6:30 Put casserole in oven.

6:35 Put cornbread in oven.

6:40 Bring water to boil in kettle.

6:45 Cook broccoli. Drain well.
Serve dinner.
When first course is finished, serve fruit.

TURKEY AND MACARONI CASSEROLE

2 cups coarsely cut cooked turkey
1 8-ounce can sliced mushrooms
3 tablespoons butter
3 tablespoons flour
1 cup chicken stock
Liquid from mushrooms
½ cup light cream
Salt and pepper to taste
8 ounces macaroni
½ cup grated cheese
Butter for dotting

Melt the 3 tablespoons butter and stir in flour smoothly. Cook, stirring constantly, for a couple of minutes. Add chicken stock, liquid from the mushrooms, and light cream and cook, stirring constantly, until thickened and smooth. Add turkey and mushrooms. Season to taste with salt and pepper. Meantime, cook macaroni in boiling, salted water 9 minutes and drain well. Line a casserole with the macaroni. Pour the turkey mixture into the center. Sprinkle cheese over and dot with butter. You may use any cheese you like— Cheddar or Parmesan are both good, for instance. Bake in 375 degree oven until golden brown (about 30 minutes). *Serves 4.*

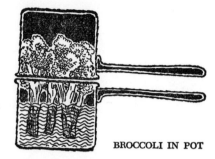

BROCCOLI IN POT

BROCCOLI 1 bunch broccoli
¼ cup (½ stick) butter, melted

Wash the broccoli well and drain. Cut off tough bottom part of stalk, leaving at least 3 inches to be cooked. Also cut off any large, tough leaves. Choose a pot in which you can stand the broccoli on its stems in tight enough formation so that it won't fall over while cooking. Pour in enough boiling water to cover the stems and not the flowers. Add a teaspoon of salt. Boil about 15 minutes, or until stems are tender. The flowers will have cooked in the steam. Drain well. Serve with melted butter poured over. *Serves 4.*

CORN BREAD 1 cup yellow cornmeal
1 cup flour
4 teaspoons baking powder
¼ cup sugar
½ teaspoon salt
1 cup milk
¼ cup melted butter
1 egg, well beaten

Mix and sift dry ingredients. Combine milk, melted butter, and egg. Add to dry ingredients slowly, beating until smooth. Bake in greased square pan in 375 degree oven 20–25 minutes. Cut in squares to serve. *Serves 4.*

BOWL OF
FRESH FRUIT

There's no more festive, beautiful, and timely centerpiece for the Thanksgiving dinner table than a generous bowl of fruit, arranged to do justice to the handsome colors and shapes available at this season. Usually, after a big turkey dinner, complete with pie for dessert, not much of the decoration is eaten on that day, so it seems fair to think that there will be plenty left for tonight's dinner. If by any chance persimmons (they're so beautiful) were part of your fruit bowl, do provide a bowl of sour cream for anyone who wants to eat them. The combination is unbeatable!

Christmas Tree-Trimming Supper

Trimming the tree on Christmas Eve is one of the nicest festivities of the season. By the time all the participants have wrapped presents and trimmed the tree they're usually good and hungry and must be fed well. But it is also wise to remember that there's a great feast coming tomorrow, so tonight's supper should be satisfying, but not too filling.

The traditional dish for Christmas Eve is oyster stew—and a cockle-warming dish it is. Nowadays, there is pretty good oyster stew in the grocer's freezer, but it's easy to make oyster stew from real fresh oysters and I give you here a recipe developed by me over years of eating in New York's Grand Central Oyster Bar. They would never tell me how to do it, so I just went time after time and observed step by step just what the men behind the counter did—and then made it and loved it, as I hope you will. In case you don't like oyster stew, I give you a recipe at the end for a very

153

easy to prepare, very good soup, all from cans, which you may use as a substitute.

On Christmas Eve in England it's traditional to serve a wassail bowl, and what could be better to provide for your tree-trimmers? In this case, the bowl consists of a delicious hot spiced cider.

SPICED CIDER WASSAIL BOWL

3 quarts cider
3 sticks cinnamon
12 whole cloves
4 allspice berries
6 tablespoons honey

Bring all ingredients to the boil. Lower heat and simmer for 15 minutes. Strain into mugs. *Makes 12 cups.*

Serve this meal in buffet fashion, the stew in a big bowl or a tureen, together with the pilot biscuits on their plate and the soup plates. Use an electric hot tray, if you have one, so that all will stay warm. Decorate the table with red candles and Christmas greens and use gay Christmas paper napkins to top it all off.

MENU
For Eight

Oyster Stew
Heated Pilot Biscuits
Caesar Salad
Golden Applesauce Cake
Coffee   Milk

Market List
1 package white cake mix
1 1-pound, 4-ounce can applesauce
1 package flaked coconut
4 dozen oysters with their juice
1 quart cream
1 package pilot biscuits
1 head iceberg lettuce
1 head romaine lettuce
¼ pound Parmesan cheese
¼ pound Blue cheese
3 quarts cider

Check These Staples
Light brown sugar (½ cup)
Butter (2½ sticks)
White raisins (1 cup)
Cinnamon
Cloves
Allspice berries
Honey
Worcestershire sauce
Celery salt
Milk (1 quart)
Paprika
White bread (4 slices)
Olive oil (¾ cup)
Garlic powder
Lemons (2 or 3)
Salt
Pepper
Egg (1)

Utensils Needed
Bowl for mixing cake
Mixing spoons
Measuring cup
Bowl for applesauce mixture
2 9"x9"x2" pans
Cooling rack
Large saucepan or casserole for stew
Cookie sheet or pan for heating pilot biscuits
Clean tea towel

Utensils
Needed
(cont.)

Skillet for frying bread cubes
Absorbent paper
Small bowl for mixing salad dressing
Cheese grater
Big salad bowl

TIMING

If supper is to be served at 8

At least a half hour before you start to pre-pare the meal, wash the lettuces, shake to remove excess moisture, wrap in a clean tea towel, and store in the refrigerator to crisp. If the cake is to be served cold, make it in the middle of the afternoon. If it is to be served warm, proceed as follows:

7:00   Make cake as directed in recipe.

7:10   Place cake in oven.

7:11   Make croutons for salad.

7:30   Make oyster stew or crab mongole. Keep warm until ready to serve.

7:35 to 7:40   Remove cake from oven. Place on rack in pans.

7:44   Place pilot biscuits in turned-off oven.

7:45   Make salad.

7:50   Turn cake out onto serving plate or plates.

8:00   Serve the supper.

After the stew and salad have been eaten, serve the cake.

GOLDEN
APPLESAUCE
CAKE

1 package white cake mix
2 cups canned applesauce

1 cup flaked coconut
½ cup light brown sugar
¼ cup melted butter
1 cup white raisins

Prepare cake mix according to directions on package. Combine applesauce, coconut, brown sugar, butter, and raisins. Pour one-half applesauce mixture into each of 2 greased 9"x9"x2" pans. Cover with cake batter divided evenly between the two pans. Bake in 375 degree oven 25–30 minutes. Cool in pans on rack for 5 minutes. Turn out upside down on cake plate or rack. Serve warm or cold.

OYSTER STEW

4 dozen oysters
½ cup butter
1 teaspoon Worcestershire Sauce
2 teaspoons celery salt
1 quart milk
1 quart cream
8 pats of butter
Paprika

Pick over oysters to make certain that there are no bits of shell present. Drain and keep the liquor. Melt the ½ cup of butter in a large saucepan or casserole. Add Worcestershire and celery salt. Add oysters and cook until they are plump and the edges curl (about 5 minutes). Add milk, cream, and oyster liquor and make very hot, but do not boil. Serve with 8 good pats of butter floating on top and a dusting of paprika. *Serves 8.*

**CAESAR
SALAD**

4 slices white bread
¼ cup olive oil
½ teaspoon garlic powder (optional)
1 head iceberg lettuce
1 head romaine lettuce
½ cup lemon juice
½ cup olive oil
Salt and pepper to taste
¼ cup freshly grated Parmesan cheese
½ cup crumbled blue cheese
1 raw egg

At least a half hour before making the salad, wash greens, shake to remove excess water, wrap in a clean tea towel, and place in the refrigerator to crisp.

Remove crusts from bread and cut each slice into cubes (about ¼" square). Heat the ¼ cup olive oil with the garlic powder in it. In this fry the bread cubes until golden and drain on absorbent paper. These are *croutons*. Tear crisped greens into a big salad bowl. Mix lemon juice and the ½ cup olive oil and season to taste. Add cheeses to the greens. Pour the lemon juice dressing over. Break the egg over the salad and toss well, so that the egg causes the cheeses to coat every piece of lettuce. Add croutons, toss again lightly. *Serves 8.*

**ALTERNATE
TO
OYSTER STEW
CRAB
MONGOLE**

2 cans condensed green pea soup
2 cans condensed tomato soup

2 cans (using soup can as measure) milk, or to taste

1 teaspoon curry powder (or more, to taste)

2 7½-ounce cans crabmeat, well picked over

Blend soups, milk, and curry powder in a saucepan. Add crabmeat. Heat, but do not boil. *Serves 8.*

Note: If you decide to use this soup, add the required ingredients to your market and staple-checking lists and remove those needed for the oyster stew.

Birthday Party

How about *your* giving a birthday party for your brother or sister, instead of letting your mother do all the work? I think you couldn't offer a more acceptable main course than pizzas, which are a justifiably popular dish among young people. Set the table attractively with a centerpiece of fresh flowers or fruits and vegetables—and carry out a color scheme of whatever is the birthday person's favorite. The birthday cake will add to this décor when it comes on with candles of the chosen color.

MENU
For Eight

Frisky Sours
Snack Crackers
Pizzas
Cooked Vegetable Salad
Strawberry Ice Cream
Angel Food Birthday Cake
Coffee   Milk

Market List
1 package angel food cake mix
Candies for decorating cake, if you're going to use them
Food coloring (for icing)
12–16 English muffins or 8 small rounds Arabic bread
Garnishes for pizza (see recipe)
½ pound mozzarella cheese
½ pound Parmesan cheese
2 10½-ounce cans pizza sauce or 2 8-ounce cans tomato sauce (with tomato bits, if obtainable)
3 packages frozen mixed vegetables
1 head Boston lettuce
3 cans condensed beef broth
2 quarts strawberry ice cream

Check These Staples
Confectioners sugar (2 or 3 cups)
Milk
Eggs (white of 1, if icing used)
Vanilla
Cream of Tartar
Sugar
Oregano
Garlic powder
Dehydrated minced onion
Olive oil
Basil
Marjoram
Bay leaf
Mayonnaise
Lemons (for ⅓ cup of juice)

Utensils Needed
Bowl for mixing cake
Angel food cake pan
Bowl for mixing icing
Bowl for mixing decorating icing, if used, plus decorating tube
Saucepan for cooking vegetables
Strainer
Bowl for chilling vegetables

Utensils	Clean tea towel
Needed	Small custard cup for olive oil
(cont.)	Pastry brush
	Cookie sheet or sheets
	Mixing spoons
	Measuring spoons
	Measuring cups
	Bowl for rehydrating onion
	Saucepan for pizza sauce
	Slicing knives
	Cheese grater
	Reamer for lemon juice
	Shaker or jar with tight-fitting lid for frisky sours

TIMING *If party is to be at 7*

In the morning (or even the night before) make the birthday cake. Frost it well in advance of starting preparation of the rest of the party.

Also in the morning, cook the vegetables, drain, cool, and chill in the refrigerator. Wash the lettuce, shake to remove excess moisture, wrap in a clean tea towel, and refrigerate.

6:00 Make the pizza sauce (when it has cooked the required short time, turn off the heat. It is not necessary that it be hot when you put it on the muffins or bread).

6:20 Grate and sliver cheeses.

6:30 Prepare whatever garnishes you've chosen (like slicing pepperoni, etc.).

6:45 Put pizzas together.

6:50 Preheat oven to 450 degrees.

6:55 Mix salad and put into lettuce-lined bowl.

7:00	Put pizzas into oven.
7:01	Shake up frisky sours and serve.
7:10 to **7:15**	Serve pizzas when they are bubbling, accompanied by the salad.

When main course is finished serve ice cream and cake, accompanied by singing "Happy Birthday to You."

**BIRTHDAY
ANGEL FOOD
CAKE**

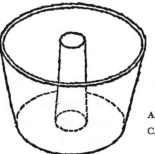

ANGEL FOOD
CAKE PAN

Angel food cake mix is one of the best of all, so by all means use one to make the birthday cake. Make it the night before or the morning of the birthday, cool it as instructed, and wrap it in plastic wrap or foil to keep it moist.

You will certainly want to decorate this cake—at least to write Happy Birthday and the name of the guest of honor on it. You can do this in one of two ways. Ice the cake and do your writing with gumdrops or other small candies, or make decorating icing and squeeze it through a decorating tube to do your writing, and perhaps other decorating as well. The plain icing which follows is fine for covering a cake, but it will not go through a tube, so there is also a recipe for decorating icing which you can use if you decide to pretty up the birthday cake that way.

PLAIN
ICING

2 cups sifted confectioners sugar
¼ cup milk
½ teaspoon vanilla

Mix all together until smooth. Spread on cake.

DECORATING
ICING

1 egg white
1 cup confectioners sugar
½ teaspoon vanilla
¼ teaspoon cream of tartar

Beat egg white, sugar, vanilla, and cream of tartar until the mixture holds stiff peaks. Tint with various colors of food coloring to use as decorations on a white-iced cake. Squeeze through a decorating tube to do your design.

COOKED
VEGETABLE
SALAD

3 packages frozen mixed vegetables
Mayonnaise (about ½ cup)
1 head Boston lettuce, washed and crisped

Cook vegetables according to package directions. Drain and chill at least two hours. Mix with mayonnaise to taste. Line a salad bowl with lettuce leaves and fill the center with vegetable salad. *Serves 8.*

PIZZAS

There are several ways you can concoct your own pizzas and have them turn out to be exceedingly good. What you use as a base is important—and I'm pretty sure you would not in the least care to make your own dough from scratch, so I will make two ready-to-go suggestions and we'll go from there. The most easily obtainable base is English muffins. But I have, from my son, discovered one which is much better, and that's Arabic bread, split in half. If you are lucky enough to live in a town which provides this bread, be sure to try it. Buy the small rounds and allow one, split in half, per person. I had hoped to be able to give you a mail-order source for this delicious bread, but discover that it will not travel well and none of the makers is willing to ship it. If you can't get it, the English muffins, also split in half, will be satisfactory. Of pizzas made with these you should allow 1½ or 2 apiece, as they are much smaller than the Arabic bread.

> 12 to 16 English muffins or 8 small rounds of Arabic bread
> ½ cup olive oil (about)
> Pizza sauce (see below)
> Garnishes: thinly sliced pepperoni, hot Italian sausage, thinly sliced onion, thinly sliced green pepper, cooked crisp bacon, canned sliced mushrooms, anchovy fillets, or what you will.
> 1 cup slivered mozzarrella cheese
> 1 cup grated Parmesan cheese

Split muffins or Arabic breads and, with a pastry brush, paint each lightly on both sides with olive oil. Place on cookie sheet or sheets. Spread a thin coating of sauce (see below) over each muffin or bread half. Add whatever you have chosen as garnish from the list above. Use at least two. Top each with a generous blanket of mozzarella, then Parmesan cheese. Bake in 450 degree oven 10–15 minutes or until bubbling. *Serves 8.*

PIZZA SAUCE

Knowing that you would probably be delighted not to bother with making your pizza sauce from scratch, I have done a bit of experimenting (with Margot's help and criticism) with a canned pizza sauce and with canned tomato sauce. We liked both, but thought perhaps the one which started as a pizza sauce was best. However, if you can't find such a sauce in your supermarket, the one based on tomato sauce comes out very well.

I   2 10½-ounce cans pizza sauce
    2 teaspoons sugar
    1 teaspoon oregano
    ¼ teaspoon garlic powder
    2 teaspoons minced onion

Heat all ingredients together in a saucepan until bubbling. Spread on whatever is your pizza base and proceed as in the pizza recipe.

II   1 tablespoon minced onion
    1 teaspoon olive oil
    2 8-ounce cans tomato sauce with tomato bits (or plain tomato sauce)
    ½ teaspoon basil
    ½ teaspoon oregano
    ¼ teaspoon marjoram

¼ teaspoon garlic powder
½ small bay leaf

Fry the minced onion in olive oil in a saucepan until golden. Add tomato sauce and seasonings and simmer gently for about 10 minutes to blend flavorings. Remove bay leaf and proceed as instructed in pizza recipe.

**FRISKY
SOURS**   3 cans condensed beef broth
¾ soup can water
12 ice cubes
⅓ cup lemon juice (or more to taste)

Put all ingredients into a shaker or a jar with a tight-fitting lid. Cover and shake well. Serve in chilled glasses. *Serves 8.*

Sunday Brunch

Next to getting your own breakfast, Sunday brunch is the easiest meal you can prepare. It's served late enough in the morning to give you plenty of relaxed preparation time. Nothing you would be likely to provide is complicated to cook, and it's easy to dream up menus for the meal which is to be the first of a two-meal day. (Of course, if hunger pangs assail you before it's dinner time you can always refer to our snack chapter and whip up a little something! Or you can eat some fruit or raw vegetables or other nutritious and nonfattening foods which will help you *hold it* until dinner is presented.)

MENU Poached Eggs on Toast
For Four Hot Barbecue Sauce
Crisp Bacon
Heated Coffee Cake
Grapefruit with Honey
Coffee   Milk

Market List	2 grapefruit
	1 coffee cake

Check These Staples	Eggs (4)
	Bread (4 slices)
	Barbecue sauce (about ¼ cup)
	Bacon (8 slices)
	Salt
	Butter
	Milk
	Coffee
	Honey
	Lemon juice or vinegar

Utensils Needed	Oblong pan with rack
	Large knife
	Grapefruit knife (or paring knife)
	Kitchen scissors (optional)
	Measuring cup
	Measuring spoons
	Heavy duty aluminum foil
	Double boiler
	Toaster
	Knife for buttering
	10" skillet
	Skimmer or slotted spoon

The pan in which I suggest you cook the bacon is usually about 10½" by 7". It can be bought with rack to fit into it. Cooking bacon on a rack allows the grease to drip down into the pan and, for this reason, the bacon needs very little draining on paper. If your kitchen has no such pan, use any rack available (like one on which you cool cake or cookies) and a pan into which it will fit.

TIMING *If brunch is to be served at 12:30*

11:30	Start oven at 200 degrees.
11:31	Place slices of bacon on rack in pan.
11:33	Start preparing grapefruit.
11:40	Place bacon in oven.

11:41 Finish preparing grapefruit. Refrigerate.

11:50 Put coffee cake into oven.

12:15 Make four pieces of toast, butter, and place in oven to keep warm.

12:20 Start water heating in skillet.

12:25 Prepare eggs according to recipe.
Serve the brunch.
When first course is finished, serve the grapefruit.

CRISP BACON

Cook 8 slices of bacon according to recipe on page 200.

GRAPEFRUIT WITH HONEY

2 grapefruit
4 tablespoons liquid honey

Cut the grapefruit in half crosswise with a large knife. Remove seeds. Cut out pithy centers of fruit with scissors, if desired (makes it easier to eat). Loosen each section of grapefruit by cutting it away from the membrane at sides and from skin at back with a grapefruit knife or a paring knife. Dribble a tablespoonful of honey over each half. Refrigerate until ready to serve.

Although one ordinarily serves fruit first at breakfast, it often provides dessert at lunch and since this meal is a combination of the two one may choose when to serve it. Your main course is what is known as a "short order" one—it has to be finished off at the last minute. Therefore it is much easier for you to serve the fruit as dessert in this instance.

COFFEE
CAKE

Some coffee cakes you might buy are packaged in aluminum pans, in which case you just remove the top of the package and heat the cake in its own pan. If you buy the cake at a bakery, wrap it in heavy-duty aluminum foil for heating.

POACHED
EGGS
ON TOAST

4 eggs
½ teaspoon salt
Few drops lemon juice or vinegar
4 slices buttered toast

Grease a 10″ skillet with butter, vegetable fat or oil (to prevent eggs from sticking). Put in about ½ inch of water. There should be just enough to cover the whites of the eggs and let the yolks stand up above it. Add salt and also lemon juice or vinegar (to help the whites coagulate). Bring to the boil. Reduce heat to a simmer. Break one egg very carefully into a tea cup and slide it into the simmering water. Do the same with each of the other three eggs in turn. Simmer very gently until the whites are done, about 2½ minutes. You can judge this by looking at the whites because they will become opaque. Also you can tell by poking them with a fork, but be careful not to break the yolks! Remove each egg gently from the water with a skimmer or a slotted spoon. Drain it thoroughly because watery eggs make toast soggy. Place each egg on a piece of toast on a heated plate. Trim the edges neatly to fit the toast. Decorate each egg with two bacon slices (cut in half if you like). Serve at once. *Serves 4.*

SKIMMER

Note: If you have a skillet with an "egg poacher" insert you may use it if you prefer. I don't like eggs done in these contraptions as well because the fact that you cover the pan when cooking makes them glaze over and I prefer bright yellow yolks.

BARBECUE SAUCE

¼ cup bottled barbecue sauce with hickory smoked flavor.

Put barbecue sauce into the top of a double boiler, cover, and place over hot water to heat. If you have no double boiler, put the sauce into a small pot and set it in a skillet of hot water. Heat at a simmer. Serve in a separate dish so that those who want some may help themselves.

FUTURES

In preparing this simple meal you have learned to poach eggs, which opens up a great variety of possibilities for luncheon and breakfast dishes. For instance, you now know how to do the hardest (not very hard!) part of making Eggs Benedict, which is a very elegant dish indeed. All you need to do is cut English muffins in half and toast them. On top of each put a warmed (easiest in a double boiler) thin slice of ham, top each with a poached egg, and pour Hollandaise sauce over all. I won't ask you to learn to make the sauce yet, but you can if you like, get in a package a rather bland dehydrated approximation of it, which you reconstitute. Or you can make all kinds of sauces to pour over eggs done in this fashion—for instance a curry sauce (see page 198) or a cheese sauce (see page 198).

Breakfast

Preparing your own breakfast is, in this cook's opinion, the first cooking thing anyone should learn to do. One major point is to give it some variety, which stimulates interest and appetite. Another is to think up quick and easy preparations which require very little work, but still give you good foods to eat. When my son was seven, I taught him to make his own breakfast. It took quite a while, but time was never better spent by me because he now had the very beginnings of knowing how to cook and he was independent of everyone else in the house in the early morning if he wanted to be. For instance, no waiting around for lazy parents on weekend mornings! Of course, one time he was preparing bacon for an overnight guest of his own age and it caught fire. This was a contingency I had not covered, so he took the pan to the sink and turned on the water. The friend dashed home in the snow, without boots or coat, terrified by the flames and smoke. But nobody was hurt. And the moral of that story is, *never* put blazing bacon into the sink. Just turn off the heat, carefully put a lid on it, and let it burn itself out! Also, if you make certain that no part of the bacon overlaps the pan even the tiniest bit, and if you cook it as it should be cooked, at a low heat, no such accident is likely to occur.

Here is a collection of suggestions for what you might prepare for yourself for breakfast, with a few tips on procedure. You can add as many variations as your imagination offers.

1. **Orange juice, cold cereal, hot muffin, milk, coffee.** The minute you get up, turn on the oven to 350 degrees and pop in a "boughten" (or leftover homemade) muffin or two.

2. **Pineapple juice, toaster waffles, maple syrup, crisp bacon** (see page 200), **milk, coffee.**

3. **Grapefruit juice, soft-cooked egg** (see page 199), **toast, jam, milk, coffee.**

4. **Applesauce, tomato, lettuce and bacon sandwich, milk, coffee.** I include the tomato, lettuce, and bacon sandwich simply to show that there's no reason why anybody shouldn't eat anything he wants to at any one meal, whether it seems odd to his grandmother or not. A nephew of mine ate this sandwich for breakfast often when he was in high school. He even added peanut butter occasionally—and loved it.

5. **Tomato juice, toaster pop-ups, scrambled eggs, milk, coffee.**
   Scrambled eggs—easiest way! Melt about 1 teaspoon butter in a small skillet over low heat. Break two eggs into pan. Stir constantly with a fork until they reach the consistency you like. Serve at once. (No egg in any style should ever be cooked at high heat. It toughens them.)

6. **Sliced orange, hot cereal** (instant), **toasted date-nut bread, milk, coffee.**

7. **Fruit cup, sausages, toaster corn sticks, hot cocoa.**
   Fruit cup: Use the canned variety which has been chilled in the refrigerator.

Sausages: Prick with a fork in a few places as many link sausages as you're prepared to eat and put into a skillet with water to cover. Boil 5 minutes. Drain off water. Return pan to low heat and brown, turning occasionally, for about 15 minutes.

Cocoa: To make one cup: mix together in a small saucepan 1 tablespoon cocoa, 1 tablespoon sugar, a dash of salt, and ¼ cup water. Bring slowly to a boil and boil gently 2 minutes. Add ¾ cup milk and heat well but *do not boil.*

8. **Half grapefruit, fried egg sandwich, milk, coffee.**

   Fried egg sandwich: Melt a teaspoon of butter in a small skillet. Break in an egg and cook over low heat until done to your taste. Turn once or serve sunny-side-up between slices of white bread or toast—with the ketchup bottle handy.

9. **Breakfast-in-one-glass, toasted raisin bread, coffee.**

   Breakfast-in-one-glass: Combine 1 can condensed tomato soup (chilled) with ½ soup can chilled orange juice, ½ soup can chilled milk, and 2 eggs. Beat with rotary beater or blend in blender. Serves 2 in tall glasses.

10. **Sliced banana, cold cereal, hot brioche** (packaged), **milk, coffee.**

Snacks—
Sweet and Savory

Everybody wants something to eat between meals at least sometimes. There are of course many packaged cookies, candies, and snack bits of the nonsweet variety available, and it's always a good idea to have some such on the kitchen shelves. On the other hand, it's also great fun to make your own, so I offer here a few suggestions of sweets and savories (nonsweet snacks) which you can whip up for yourself, or with your friends—and enjoy the more because you made them.

Sweet Snacks

SUGAR ON SNOW

This recipe comes from Vermont, where my friend Margot goes often. If you're where there's lots of nice clean snow on the ground, pack some of it very firmly into a pan so that it is good and solid, then proceed as in the recipe below with your boiled maple syrup. But if you're a liver-in-the-city or home is in a hot climate, do it this way:

> 1 ice tray full of water (no divider in it)
> ½ cup maple syrup

Freeze an ice tray full of water. When this is done bring the maple syrup to a full boil and boil about 5–6 minutes, until it is thickened. Meantime, shave the top of the ice in your tray so that it makes a little "snow" (is roughened up a little). With a spoon, pour the syrup onto the ice in round blobs about the size of a fifty-cent piece. This will quickly harden into thin, crisp pieces. *Makes 10–12.*

If you don't eat all the sugar-on-snow immediately, leave the pieces on the ice and put it back into the freezer. If you take them off the ice and put them onto plastic wrap, then wrap them up in it securely. You can keep them in the freezer beautifully. Of course the likelihood is that they will be consumed at once and there will be no keeping problems!

OVENLESS COOKIES

1 cup sugar
3 tablespoons cocoa
½ cup instant nonfat dry milk
2 tablespoons butter
¼ cup water
¼ cup peanut butter
1½ cups rolled oats
1 teaspoon vanilla

Mix sugar, cocoa, milk, butter, and water in a pan. Bring to a boil. Stir and boil 2 minutes. Remove from heat and add peanut butter. Stir until peanut butter is melted. Add rolled oats. Add vanilla. Mix well. Drop by spoonfuls on waxed paper. Let cool at room temperature before serving or storing. *Makes 24 1½-inch cookies.*

Check These Staples	Sugar (1 cup)
	Cocoa (3 tablespoons)
	Instant nonfat dry milk (½ cup)
	Butter
	Peanut butter (¼ cup)
	Rolled oats (1½ cups)
	Vanilla
Utensils Needed	Measuring cups
	Measuring spoons
	Saucepan
	Stirring and mixing spoon
	Waxed paper

GLAZED NO-BAKE BROWNIES

4 cups graham cracker crumbs

1 cup chopped walnuts

½ cup unsifted confectioners sugar

1 package (8 squares) semisweet chocolate squares

¾ cup evaporated milk

1 teaspoon vanilla

¼ cup evaporated milk

Combine crumbs, nuts, and sugar in a large bowl. Place chocolate and the ¾ cup of evaporated milk in a small saucepan over low heat. Heat, stirring constantly, until chocolate is melted and smooth. Remove from heat. Stir in vanilla. Measure ½ cup and set aside for use as glaze. Stir the ¼ cup evaporated milk into the remaining chocolate mixture. Stir into crumb mixture. Grease a 9-inch square pan lightly. Spread mixture evenly into it. Spread reserved chocolate mixture over the top. Chill until ready to serve. Cut into small bars. *Makes about 32 bars.*

Market List	10 ounces (approximately) graham cracker crumbs
	¼ pound, plus, walnuts
	1 package semisweet chocolate squares
Check These Staples	Confectioners sugar (½ cup)
	Evaporated milk (1 cup)
	Vanilla
Utensils Needed	Large bowl
	Small saucepan
	Stirring spoon
	Measuring cups
	Measuring spoons
	9-inch square pan
	Knife for cutting bars

CHOCOLATE MORSEL COOKIES

½ cup (1 stick) butter, softened
¼ cup granulated sugar
½ cup brown sugar
1 egg, beaten
1 cup, plus 2 level tablespoons sifted flour
½ teaspoon soda

½ teaspoon salt
½ teaspoon vanilla
½ cup chopped pecans (or other nuts)
1 cup (1 6-ounce package) chocolate morsels

Soften butter by leaving it at room temperature for at least a half hour. Beat until creamy. Add the two sugars gradually and beat until very light and fluffy. Add well-beaten egg and beat again. Sift flour with salt and soda and add to the first mixture. Add vanilla, nuts, and chocolate morsels. Mix thoroughly. Drop from the tip of a teaspoon on lightly greased cookie sheets (about 2 inches apart). Bake in 375 degree oven until delicately browned (10–12 minutes). *Makes about 50 cookies.*

Market List
1 6-ounce package chocolate morsels
¼ pound nut meats (This is more than you need, but about as little as you can buy.)

Check These Staples
Butter (1 stick)
Granulated sugar (¼ cup)
Brown sugar (½ cup)
Eggs (1)
Flour
Soda
Salt
Vanilla

Utensils Needed
Bowl for beating batter
Small bowl for beating egg
Flour sifter
Measuring cups
Measuring spoons
Cookie sheets

COOKIE
CONFECTIONS

1 cup (1 6-ounce package) butterscotch morsels
2 cups chow mein noodles
1 cup dry roasted peanuts without skins

Melt morsels over hot water. Remove from heat and stir in noodles and nuts. Drop by teaspoonfuls onto cookie sheets covered with waxed paper. Refrigerate until set. Store in a tightly covered tin in the refrigerator. They can keep several weeks, but of course they won't. They can also be frozen. *Makes about 3 dozen.*

Market List
1 6-ounce package butterscotch morsels
5 ounces chow mein noodles
1 jar dry roasted peanuts without skins (you need 1 cup)

Utensils Needed
Measuring cups
Double boiler
Stirring spoon
Teaspoon
Cookie sheets

CHOCOLATE
FUDGE

2 squares unsweetened chocolate
⅔ cup milk
2 cups sugar
Dash salt
2 tablespoons butter
1 teaspoon vanilla

Add chocolate to milk and cook over low heat, stirring constantly, until mixture is smooth and blended. Add sugar and salt and stir until sugar is dissolved and mixture boils. Cook, stirring constantly, until a small amount of the mixture forms a soft ball when dropped into cold water (236 degrees on the candy thermometer). Remove from heat. Add butter and vanilla without stirring. Cool until it is lukewarm (110 degrees on candy thermometer), then beat until creamy (easiest with an electric mixer). Turn at once into a greased pan. When firm, cut into squares. *Makes about 18 large pieces.* **Note:** You may add ¾ cup chopped nuts or 1 cup tiny marshmallows just before turning fudge into the pan if you like.

Check These Staples	Unsweetened chocolate (2 squares)
	Milk (⅔ cup)
	Sugar (2 cups)
	Salt
	Butter
	Vanilla
Utensils Needed	Measuring cups
	Measuring spoons
	Saucepan
	Stirring spoon
	Candy thermometer
	Electric mixer or hand beater
	Square or oblong pan

PULLED TAFFY

A taffy pull is fun on a rainy afternoon when you "can't think of anything to do." And the taffy is fun to eat any time at all.

1 cup granulated sugar
½ cup brown sugar
2 cups molasses
¾ cup water
¼ cup (½ stick) butter
¼ teaspoon baking soda
¼ teaspoon salt

Boil sugars, molasses, and water until a small amount of the mixture cracks when dropped into cold water (265 degrees on candy thermometer). Remove from heat. Add butter, baking soda, and salt and stir to mix. Pour into a greased large platter and allow to stand until cool enough to handle. Dip fingers into oil (the buttery flavored kind is good for this) and gather the taffy into a ball. Pull, using the tips of your fingers, until candy is firm and light colored. You may add peppermint or other flavoring during the pulling and a bit of vegetable coloring. Stretch the taffy out into a long rope and twist it slightly. Cut into 1-inch lengths with scissors dipped frequently into cold water. *Makes about 50 pieces.*

Check These Staples	Granulated sugar (1 cup) Brown sugar (½ cup) Molasses (2 cups) Butter (½ stick) Baking soda Salt Buttery flavored oil for hands Flavorings (if desired) Vegetable coloring (if desired)
Utensils Needed	Saucepan Candy thermometer Stirring spoon Large platter Scissors for cutting candy into lengths

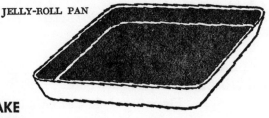

JELLY-ROLL PAN

NO-BAKE CHOCOLATE PEANUT BITES

½ cup sugar
½ cup light corn syrup
¾ cup peanut butter
½ teaspoon vanilla
3 cups corn flakes
2 cups semisweet chocolate morsels

Mix sugar and corn syrup in a saucepan and bring to the boil. Remove from heat and add peanut butter, vanilla and cereal. Spread on a greased jelly-roll pan (a cookie sheet with sides) and pat out evenly with your hands. Melt chocolate morsels and spread over the top with a spatula. Refrigerate. Break into bite-sized pieces to serve. *Makes about 3 dozen.*

Market List	2 6-ounce packages semisweet chocolate morsels
Check These Staples	Sugar (½ cup) Light corn syrup (½ cup) Peanut butter (¾ cup) Vanilla Cornflakes (3 cups)
Utensils Needed	Saucepan Mixing spoon Jelly-roll pan Double boiler for melting chocolate Spatula

Milk Shakes, Frosteds and Sodas

BASIC
MILK SHAKE
2 cups chilled milk
Flavoring of choice (see below)

Combine milk and flavoring and beat with a rotary beater, or shake vigorously in a shaker or, easiest and best, whirl in the blender. *Serves 2.*

Chocolate: Add ¼ cup instant cocoa or ¼ cup chocolate syrup to milk. Blend well. Taste and add more flavoring if desired.

Banana: Add 1 small banana, mashed, and a dash of sugar.

Orange: Add 4 cups orange juice, ¼ cup sugar, and a dash of salt to milk, plus 1 cup of crushed ice. *Serves 6.*

Strawberry or Raspberry: Add ¼ cup strawberry or raspberry syrup to milk.

Mocha: Add ⅓ cup of very strong cold coffee to chocolate milkshake mixture before blending.

Pineapple: Add ½ cup sweetened pineapple juice to milk.

Apricot: Add ¼ cup apricot nectar to milk.

Vanilla: Add 2 teaspoons vanilla extract to milk. Blend. Taste and add more flavoring if desired.

Egg: The addition of a raw egg for every 2 cups of milk used makes the milkshakes more fluffy and also more nutritious.

FROSTED

To turn a milk shake into a frosted, add a scoop of ice cream of any flavor you fancy to any milk shake before blending. You may also add another scoop to the glass before pouring in the liquid if you like. Serve long spoons with this kind.

SODAS

Make your frosted and pour into tall glasses, until about ¾ full. Fill up with club soda and stir only enough to mix.

GRAHAM CRACKER CRISPIES

24 graham crackers
½ cup (1 stick) butter
¾ cup firmly packed light brown sugar
½ cup chopped nuts

Butter 15½"x10½"x1" jelly-roll pan. Place crackers in it in a single layer. In a saucepan combine butter and sugar. Cook over medium heat, stirring constantly, until sugar dissolves. Spread over crackers, sprinkle with nuts. Bake in 350 degree oven 10 minutes. Cool in pan on a wire rack. When cool, cut into rectangular pieces. *Makes 48.*

Market List
Graham crackers (24)
¼ pound nuts (This is more than you need for ½ cup, but as little as you can buy.)

Check These Staples
Butter (1 stick)
Light brown sugar (¾ cup, firmly packed)

Utensils Needed
Jelly-roll pan (see above for size)
Saucepan
Stirring spoon
Wire rack

GINGER COOKIES

2 cups sifted flour
½ teaspoon baking powder
¼ teaspoon baking soda
1 teaspoon ground ginger
½ teaspoon salt
½ cup (1 stick) butter
½ cup sugar
½ cup molasses
1 egg
2 tablespoons water

Mix and sift 1½ cups of the flour with the baking powder, soda, ginger, and salt. Cream butter (see page 9) until soft. Beat in sugar, molasses, egg, and water. Stir in flour mixture, then gradually add remaining flour until dough is just stiff enough to roll. Chill thoroughly. Place on lightly floured board (covered with pastry cloth, if available) and roll ⅛ inch thick. Cut with cutter dipped in flour as desired and placed on ungreased cookie sheet. Bake in 375 degree oven 8 to 10 minutes. *Makes about 5 dozen cookies.*

Check These Staples

Flour (2 cups)
Baking powder
Baking soda
Ground ginger
Salt
Butter (1 stick)
Sugar
Molasses (½ cup)
Eggs (1)

Utensils Needed

Flour sifter
Bowl for mixing
Mixing spoon

Pastry board and cloth
Rolling pin
Cutter or cutters
Cookie sheet or sheets

Savory Snacks

CHEESE DREAMS

When I was in my teens I had a passion for making myself cheese dreams as an evening snack. My father, observing this phenomenon, would say to me, "If you eat that at this hour you'll see your grandmother in the middle of the night," meaning that I'd have nightmares. Well, I didn't, but his implication was perhaps wise and a cheese dream is probably a better afternoon snack than an evening one.

    4 slices white bread
    2 slices Cheddar cheese
    4 tablespoons butter

Place a slice of cheese between each two slices of bread. Spread the top slices with a tablespoon of butter each. Melt the remaining butter in a skillet and place the Dreams in it, buttered side up. Cook over low heat until bread is golden brown. Turn and brown second sides. Low heat is required so that the cheese may melt. Makes two Dreams.

Check These
Staples
White bread (4 slices)
Cheddar cheese
Butter (½ stick)

Utensils	Knife for buttering
Needed	Skillet
	Pancake turner

HOT
SOUP

A bowl of hot soup is a cockle-warming and delicious snack. If you like some canned soups just as they come, see that there's a good assortment available. One can, diluted as directed, serves two or three. If there's any left over, store it, covered, in the refrigerator for another's day's snack. It's also fun to mix soups. Here are some possibilities:

Bean with Bacon, plus Vegetable Beef, plus 2 cans water
Beef, plus Tomato, plus 1½ cans water
Bisque of Tomato, plus Chicken Gumbo, plus 1½ cans water
Black Bean, plus Beef Broth, plus 1½ cans water
Chicken Gumbo, plus Cream of Chicken, plus 2 cans milk
Chicken Noodle, plus Vegetable, plus 1½ cans water
Chicken and Stars, plus Cream of Chicken, plus 1½ cans
    water
Chili Beef, plus Vegetable, plus 2 cans water
Clam Chowder, plus Vegetarian Vegetable, plus 2 cans water
Consommé, plus Tomato, plus 1 can water
Cream of Potato, plus Chicken Vegetable, plus 1½ to 2 cans
    water
Noodles and Ground Beef, plus Onion, plus 2 cans water
Split Pea with Ham, plus Old-Fashioned Vegetable, plus 1½
    cans water
Turkey Vegetable, plus Chicken Noodle, plus 1½ cans water
Vegetable Bean, plus Tomato, plus 1½ cans water
Frozen Cream of Potato, plus Frozen Oyster Stew, plus 1½
    cans milk

Frozen Cream of Shrimp, plus Frozen Cream of Potato, plus a can each of water and milk

Frozen Green Pea with Ham, plus Frozen Cream of Potato, plus 2 cans water

Frozen New England Clam Chowder, plus Frozen Cream of Potato, plus a can each of water and milk

Frozen Oyster Stew, plus Frozen Green Pea with Ham, plus 1½ cans milk

RAW VEGETABLES

Especially if you're watching your weight, raw vegetables offer one of the lowest calorie, good-for-you snacks imaginable. Every two or three days prepare some, scraping and cutting as necessary, put them into a bowl of ice water in the refrigerator, always ready for that moment when you're so hungry you just have to have something to munch on, but don't want whatever it is to be fattening. Good vegetables for this purpose are: carrots, sweet peppers, celery, cauliflower flowerets, broccoli flowerets, scallions, radishes, cucumber, and Belgian endive and, for that matter, any vegetable you like to eat raw. Plain salt or seasoned salt are good for dipping these foods into before nibbling.

BOUILLON ON THE ROCKS

This is another nourishing calorie-saver. And it's refreshing in either hot or cold weather, too. I like to pour the canned bouillon over ice with no dilution beyond that which the ice cubes provide. Canned bouillon is a good kitchen shelf staple, so try to be sure there are always a few cans available.

POPCORN

There are three possible ways to make popcorn. First, if you're lucky enough to have a fireplace, it's fun to use a wire popper over the living room fire. Do not put in too much corn at once or the last part of the batch will not have room to pop. Shake the popper constantly, not too near the fire or you'll burn it. Then, you can pop corn in a frying pan. In this case, you melt two tablespoons of butter in the pan and add ¼ to ½ cup of corn, depending upon the size of the pan. Cover the pan and shake over low heat until the corn is all popped. Last, there's the electric popper which gives excellent results, but is perhaps not as much fun as one of the do-it-yourself methods. Follow the directions which come with any electric popper. When the corn is popped by any method, empty it into a bowl and add salt and melted butter to taste, stirring gently to reach all the popcorn.

> **1 cup of popping corn will give you 5 cups of popped corn.**

CHEESE
STICKS

6 slices white bread
½ cup (1 stick) butter
1 cup grated Parmesan cheese

Cut crusts from bread. Cut slices into four fingers each. Spread cheese on a plate or platter. Melt butter in a skillet. Dip each bread finger quickly into the butter. Roll in the grated cheese. Place on an ungreased cookie sheet. Bake in 250 degree oven until golden brown (45–60 minutes). *Makes 24 sticks.*

Market List	¼ pound Parmesan cheese
Check These Staples	White bread (6 slices) Butter (1 stick)
Utensils Needed	Knife to cut bread Cheese grater Skillet Cookie sheet

HARD-COOKED EGGS

Hard-cooked eggs (see page 199) make tasty and filling snack food and if you cook a couple and refrigerate them, you may like to eat one between meals on a day when there are no other eggs in the family menus.

CHICKEN WINGS

1 pound chicken wings
2 tablespoons butter
¼ cup grated Parmesan cheese
1½ teaspoons chopped fresh parsley
1 teaspoon oregano
¼ teaspoon salt
Dash pepper

Cut tips from chicken wings and throw them away. Cut the wings in half at the joint, making 2 pieces of each. (This is most easily done with a cleaver if you have one. Otherwise use a heavy, sharp knife. Not hard to do in any case.) Melt butter. Mix remaining ingredients. Dip wings into butter, then in cheese mixture. Line a shallow baking pan with foil. Lay the wing pieces in it. Drizzle over them any remaining butter. Bake in 350 degree oven 1 hour. These are exceedingly good hot or cold. *This amount makes enough snack food for six.*

Market List	1 pound chicken wings Fresh parsley
Check These Staples	Butter Parmesan cheese (¼ cup, grated) Oregano Salt Pepper
Utensils Needed	Cleaver or heavy sharp knife Skillet for melting butter Plate for cheese mixture Shallow baking pan Foil

Basic Recipes

CREAM SAUCE
Or White Sauce

Thin
1 tablespoon butter
1 tablespoon flour
1 cup milk
1 teaspoon salt

Medium
2 tablespoons butter
2 tablespoons flour
1 cup milk
1 teaspoon salt

Thick
3 tablespoons butter
3 tablespoons flour
1 cup milk
1 teaspoon salt

Melt butter in a small saucepan. Stir in flour smoothly. Cook for about a minute, stirring constantly. Add milk gradually and cook, *stirring constantly,* until thickened and smooth. Add salt and stir well.

The constant stirring prevents lumps, which will certainly appear if you don't heed the instruction.

Use cream sauce on potatoes or other vegetables, as the basic sauce for a casserole, for chicken, for hard-cooked eggs, or for fish.

The French call this a Bechamel sauce. It may also be made with 1 cup of chicken stock instead of the milk and with a couple of tablespoons of cream added at the end.

From this most basic of sauces you can make quite a variety of others:

Curry Sauce: When you make a medium cream sauce add from 1 teaspoon to 1 tablespoon of curry powder along with the flour required in the recipe. Use with meat, poultry, or vegetables.

Cheese Sauce: Make a thin cream sauce. Add ½ cup grated Cheddar, Swiss, or Parmesan cheese and stir constantly until entirely melted and incorporated into the sauce. You may, instead, add ¼ cup of Swiss and ¼ cup of Parmesan. The French call this Mornay sauce.

Paprika Sauce: Make a Bechamel sauce with chicken stock and cream and add at least a tablespoonful of paprika when you put in the flour required in the recipe. This is a Hungarian sauce and should be a good pink color. Use with chicken or veal.

Mushroom Sauce: Make a thick cream sauce and add to it a 4-ounce can of sliced mushrooms with their juice. Stir until well incorporated. Use with chicken or turkey, with eggs, or with vegetables. It is particularly good with spinach.

HARD-
COOKED
EGGS 2 or more eggs

In a saucepan the right size to hold the number of eggs you're going to cook place the eggs and cover them *entirely* with cold water. Bring to the boil over high heat. Remove at once from the heat, cover the pan and let stand 20 minutes. Pour off hot water and run cold water over eggs to stop cooking and cool, prevent a dark surface on the yolks, and make the shells easier to remove. Mark with an x in pencil to identify them. Chill in the refrigerator. When ready to use, crackle the shells on a hard surface. Roll eggs between your hands to loosen the shells, then peel. Holding the eggs under running cold water while easing off the shell sometimes helps, too.

SOFT
COOKED
EGGS 2 or more eggs

Put eggs into a saucepan and cover with cold water to cover them *entirely*. Bring water to the boil over high heat. Cover and remove from heat at once. Set timer for 3 minutes. When it rings, run cold water over the eggs to stop cooking and make them cool enough on the outside for you to open them comfortably.

SEPARATING
EGG YOLKS
FROM WHITES

Tap the eggs sharply midway between the ends on the edge of a bowl to crack it. With the fingers, break it into two halves, holding them upright over the bowl you have chosen for the whites. Let the white drop into the bowl, working the yolk back and forth between the two shell halves until all the white is in its bowl. Place yolk in a small bowl. If *any* trace of yolk gets into the whites you must remove it or the whites will not beat properly. Do this with a teaspoon or with a piece of paper toweling.

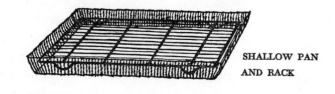

SHALLOW PAN
AND RACK

CRISP
BACON   8 slices of bacon, separated

The bacon is easier to separate if you take it out of the refrigerator a half hour before you mean to cook it. Lay slices of bacon on rack in a shallow oblong pan. Cook in 200 degree oven for 45 minutes. The slow cooking prevents it from curling up. When it is done drain briefly on paper toweling. Because of the rack, there won't be much fat to drain off.

If you prefer, you can fry the bacon in a skillet. Use *very* low heat, again, so it won't curl. It should take 30–45 minutes to be brown and crisp. Turn occasionally. Drain on paper toweling.

FRENCH
DRESSING   6 tablespoons olive oil
2 tablespoons vinegar or lemon juice
½ teaspoon salt
Dash of pepper

Mix all together well and pour over salad. Toss or not as the recipe directs. *Enough for 6.*

The proper proportion for French dressing is three table-spoons oil to one of lemon juice or vinegar, as illustrated above.

The French call this a Sauce Vinaigrette.

WHIPPED CREAM

½ pint heavy cream

1 teaspoon superfine sugar *or* ½ teaspoon salt

Beat cream and sugar or salt (depending upon what you're going to use it for) with an electric or a rotary beater to the thickness you desire. The big thing to be careful about is that you don't beat the cream too much (it would turn to butter). Stop every now and then and lift the cream with the beater to discover the consistency. When it is nearly ready you will see swirls on top as you beat.

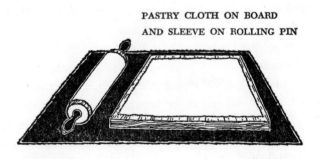

PASTRY CLOTH ON BOARD
AND SLEEVE ON ROLLING PIN

SUGAR COOKIES

In order to make these basic cookies you must learn to use a rolling pin. The greatest difficulty in this process for beginning cooks is that the dough is likely to stick to the rolling pin and the board on which you're rolling it. Of course you are told to "flour" the board and the pin, but there's an almost infallible solution to the problem which is to put a pastry cloth on the board and a "sleeve" on the rolling pin, then flour each lightly. The dough just doesn't stick. The cloths and sleeves are sold in sets in housewares departments and stores, and I do hope you can acquire a set if it's not already in your kitchen.

2 cups sifted flour
1½ teaspoons baking powder
½ teaspoon salt
½ cup butter
1 cup sugar
1 egg
1 teaspoon vanilla
1 tablespoon milk
sugar for sprinkling

The easiest way to sift flour into cup measurements, as required here, is to have one of those small hand-sifters, the bottom of which fits into a measuring cup neatly. With a big, old-fashioned sifter it's possible but much harder. Mix and sift sifted flour, baking powder, and salt. Cream butter (see page 9) until soft. Beat in sugar, egg, vanilla, and milk. Add to flour mixture, mixing well. Wrap the dough in foil or plastic wrap and chill thoroughly (at least 30 minutes). Place on lightly floured board (or pastry cloth on board) and roll out to ⅛ inch thick. Cut with cutter, dipped in flour, as desired and place on an ungreased baking sheet. Sprinkle with sugar and bake in 375 degree oven about 10 minutes. Makes 4–5 dozen cookies. Decorate as desired.

SMALL HAND SIFTER

Things you can do with this recipe:

Butterscotch Cookies: Use ½ cup firmly packed brown sugar instead of the sugar required in the basic recipe.

Spice Sugar Cookies: Add ¼ teaspoon *each* cinnamon, allspice, and cloves to flour mixture before sifting.

Chocolate Cookies: Melt 2 squares unsweetened chocolate and add to butter mixture before adding dry ingredients.

Nut Cookies: Add ½ cup chopped nuts to the flour mixture.

Raisin Cookies: Add ½ cup chopped raisins to flour mixture. Or use chopped dates, currants, or apricots.

Decorate the cookies with frosting or anything else that suits your fancy or is appropriate to the occasion upon which you wish to serve them.

ICING 1 egg white
1 teaspoon vanilla
1 cup powdered sugar (about)

Beat egg white until frothy but not stiff. Sprinkle vanilla over and gradually beat in sugar until icing is stiff enough to spread. Will ice 20 cup cakes—or decorate a lot of cookies. **Bonuses:** This icing may be tinted with vegetable coloring to match up with any special event party you may wish to give. Divide it into several bowls and color it with various colors if you like.

The icing can also be flavored in several ways: substitute lemon juice, pineapple juice, or orange juice for the vanilla, or use almond essence for a sophisticated flavor.

FUTURES

Once you have learned to use a rolling pin, as in the recipe for sugar cookies, you will then be able to make pastry, or pie crust, which opens up many new fields for you to conquer.

Setting the Table

The simplest of table settings is what you want for any of the meals you're likely to cook. As a matter of fact, in today's world it's what almost everybody wants for any meal at all. The fact that practically no one has any kind of outside help in the home has simplified many things—and in my opinion that's all to the good.

For a seated breakfast, lunch, or dinner follow these basic rules. The knife goes to the right of the plate with the cutting edge toward the plate. Spoons, in the order in which they will be used, working from the outside in, are placed to the right of the knife. For instance, if you will need a soup spoon, and a teaspoon for dessert, the soup spoon goes on the outside and the teaspoon next to the knife. Forks are placed to the left of the plate in the order in which they are to be used, again working from the outside in. For instance, if you are providing a dinner fork and a salad fork, the dinner fork is on the outside and the salad fork next to the plate, unless you follow the California custom of serving salad as a first course, in which case the salad fork is on the outside!

The ends of the handles of all knives, forks, and spoons are

TABLE SETTING

lined up evenly with the place where the bottom of the plate will be. Butter knives are put on the plate any way you like, provided they are in the same position on each plate at the table. Across the top of the butter plate, as illustrated here, is the most usual and convenient arrangement.

The water glasses are placed just above the tip of each knife. If there are also glasses of milk, they go to the right of the water glasses.

Napkins can be placed either to the left of the fork or to the right of the knife and spoons. You will find as many "experts" (if you care) who insist on one as on the other. I prefer the napkin to the right of the knife and spoons because, being right-handed, I find it much easier to pick up and put in my lap than reaching across to the left would be. The napkins should be simply folded; either in a triangle, with the longest side next to the silver and the point away from it, or in an oblong, with the fold toward the silver.

When you set the table always remember the salts and peppers. I hope you have pepper mills—freshly ground pepper is so much better than the ready-ground variety.

The centerpiece on your table can be anything attractive

that you want it to be. A bowl of fruit or vegetables is appetizing and handsome. Flowers are always lovely. Perhaps you have some ceramic objects which would look well as a dining-table decoration. In any event, remember that any dining table needs a focal point of interest and color.

Whether you use a tablecloth or mats depends on what you have available.

If there is a first course in the meal you're serving, it may be ready at each place when the participants appear at the table.

FOR THE BUFFET PARTY

As is true of table setting for seated meals, your greatest endeavor should be to have things neat, handy, and never, never tricky. The "correct" way to set any table is to make the guests as comfortable and happy as possible. A sense of order about the way the table looks helps in that connection.

So! Set your buffet table either with a large cloth to cover it completely or have it bare. Mats slip about too much and look choppy. If the table is in the center of the room, there should be a decoration of some sort in the center of the table, but never so big that it interferes with people's serving themselves. If you prefer to push the table against the wall the decoration can then go at the back against the wall.

Always arrange food and accessories so that they are most convenient for your guests. Have the hot plates where people will start serving themselves. Then arrange the food on its serving platters or plates in some logical sequence, proper serving pieces beside each, with the bread to be taken last and the necessary silver—forks and knives, if essential—and napkins neatly laid out for people to pick up as they head for wherever they will enjoy the meal. Clear everything away (except in the case of a Smörgåsbord) before producing the dessert and the necessary spoons and forks with which it will be eaten.

Index

CHARLOTTE ADAMS has been Food Editor of the Associated Press, *Look*, *Collier's* and *Charm* Magazines. She has written many cookbooks, but this is her first for young people. She brings to it not only her cooking knowledge and experience, but an admiration and understanding for youth. She says that this was greatly enhanced by her years as a member of the staff and board of the Child Study Association of America and, most importantly, by her son who is a gifted cook and her three grandsons who are "the greatest thing that ever happened to me" and who love to eat!